Social AI Revolution

Revolution

Winning Tactics for the Smart Content Creator

By
Nathan Venture D

To You,

Thank you!

Table of Contents

Introduction

In an era where the digital landscape is continuously undergoing rapid transformation, the confluence of Artificial Intelligence and social media stands as a beacon for a revolutionary shift in how content is created, managed, and consumed. Content creators, marketers, digital strategists, and professionals alike are witnessing an age where the art of communication is no longer just about creativity but also about the symbiotic relationship with technology. This book is your compass in navigating the vibrant yet mystifying realm of social AI content creation.

The allure of AI for social media isn't just in its ability to streamline processes or provide analytics. It's about the expansive potential that comes with automating creativity, personalizing experiences to the individual consumer, and crafting messages that strike a chord across diverse audiences. This introductory segment doesn't just serve as a preamble; it is the beginning of a journey that will shape the way you think about, interact with, and ultimately harness the power of Artificial Intelligence in the context of social media.

We stand on the precipice of an AI-driven revolution that is reshaping the marketing and content creation arenas. As you traverse this landscape, it's essential to understand not just the "how" but the "why" behind employing AI in social media strategies. AI isn't just a tool; it's a dynamic partner—one that can anticipate trends, generate compelling narratives, and engage with users on a level that feels immensely human.

By integrating AI into your social media strategies, you create a bridge between raw data and human emotion, where algorithms comprehend the heartbeat of social discourse. AI tools have started to redefine what it means to be creative, to be engaging, and to be responsive to the ever-changing tastes and preferences of a global audience. In the coming chapters, we'll delve into the essentials of AI-enabled content creation, but for now, let us whet your appetite with a glimpse into the immense possibilities that await.

The digital age has often been likened to a vast sea, with currents and options as numerous as they are unpredictable. In this scenario, AI represents both a compass and a rudder, guiding content creators through uncharted waters and offering them the means to navigate with confidence. The strategies you will encounter in these pages are your maps charted by the stars of advanced algorithms and machine learning capabilities.

As we embark on this exploration, it's important to acknowledge the inherent power of personalization. In the coming chapters, personalized content creation through AI will be a recurring theme, demonstrating not just the importance of speaking directly to your audience's interests and needs, but also the unmatched efficiency with which AI can segment, target, and engage individuals at scale.

Yet, with such power comes responsibility. Our journey will not shy away from the ethical considerations that arise in the wake of AI's capabilities. As you learn to navigate the AI landscape, you must also become a steward of ethical content creation, ensuring transparency, fairness, and respect for the intellectual property of both humans and AI.

The integration of AI into social media is not without its hurdles—changes in technology, platform algorithms, and user behavior patterns are but a few factors that require vigilance and adaptability. The tactics outlined herein will aid you in not just adapting to change but embracing and anticipating it, positioning you as a forerunner in the social AI field.

Digital storytelling is evolving, and AI tools are the new brushes and palettes at your disposal. Whether you are creating visually stunning posts or compelling written narratives, AI can help amplify your natural creativity, bringing a depth and insight to your content that is intuitive and yet, ineffably precise. The key to leveraging these tools lies in the mastery of best practices for tool adoption, an expertise that you will develop in the chapters to follow.

For your content to not just reach but resonate with audiences, AI can play a pivotal role in content distribution. Timing, as you know, is everything. In the nuanced world of social media, AI's predictive analysis can make the difference between a message that flourishes and one that fades away without a trace. Discover how to optimize your content's visibility and impact with AI-driven scheduling techniques.

Akin to the pied piper, AI can lead the way in building communities and engaging audiences with a level of sophistication that elevates user experiences from transactional to transformational. Learn how AI's analytical prowess can convert passive viewers into active participants and advocates of your brand.

Measurable success is the yardstick by which we evaluate strategy effectiveness. In later discussions, we will explore how AI augments analytics and reporting, equipping you with sharper tools to interpret data and adapt your strategies effectively. Yet, in this introduction, the groundwork is laid for understanding that without a bedrock of goals and success metrics, even the most sophisticated AI tools can't bring about the desired outcomes.

Finally, as you endeavor to make your mark in the burgeoning nexus of AI and social media, it's pivotal to embrace a mindset of continuous learning and skill refinement. The AI landscape does not stand still, and nor should you. By preparing yourself to pivot and proceed with the agility that the digital era demands, you ensure that your skills remain as relevant and potent as the technology you wield.

It's time to embark on this transformative journey. Ready your canvas and palette— let us paint a future where AI and human ingenuity merge in a masterpiece of engaging, personalized, and ethically-crafted social media content.

Chapter 1:
The Dawn of the Social AI Era

In the tapestry of today's digital communication, a new thread is being interwoven, marking the emergence of an epoch where artificial intelligence not only supports but actively participates in the exchange of social narratives. Far from being a whispered prophecy on the fringes of technology forums, this era has arrived with a promise of transformation. It steers us away from the traditional battlements from where we've waged our campaigns for audience engagement and propels us into a dynamic dance with algorithms that learn, interpret, and evoke. Here, at the dawn of the Social AI era, we unfold the story of this unprecedented ally to marketers and content creators. Through the illumination of AI's gradually complex role within social platforms, we witness a reinvention of engagement strategies, a reshaping of community interactions, and a redefining of content relevance. As we stand on the cusp of this new horizon, it's imperative to grasp the essence of Social AI—not merely as tools and automations, but as the bedrock for a revolution that's setting the stage for a future where every social gesture is amplified by intelligent, analytical, and adaptive technology.

Understanding Social AI

Delving into the realm of Social AI, one must grasp that this technology transcends traditional algorithms, embodying the nuanced ability to discern, learn from, and engage with human social behavior. It's here where artificial intelligence meets the hustle of social media, navigating the streams of trending topics, emotions, and viral content with unprecedented finesse. As marketers and content creators on the threshold of innovation, acknowledging the fine-tuned capabilities of Social AI becomes crucial—it's not just about analyzing data, but about crafting experiences that feel uniquely personal and deeply resonant. Envision a tool that doesn't replace the human touch but magnifies it, empowering your voice to echo across diverse demographics and psychographics. The insights gleaned from Social AI are potent; they equip one with the foresight to anticipate audience reactions, tailor conversations, and cultivate a digital presence that's both influential and authentic. For those ready to wield this transformative power, it's imperative to command a clear understanding of this digital symbiosis—it's how you'll spearhead content that doesn't just speak to an audience, but speaks them.

The Evolution of Artificial Intelligence in Social Media

The trajectory of artificial intelligence in social media presents a riveting evolution. It has progressed from being an obscure and rarely understood technology to an integral component of the social media landscape that we interact with daily. In an industry that constantly hungers for innovation, AI has certainly been a game-changer—refining tools, analytics, and functionalities that seem to almost foresee our needs and preferences.

Let's navigate through time and look at the shape-shifting silhouette of AI within social media. The rudimentary algorithms first deployed were largely focused on basic tasks like filtering spam and recommending friends. But as our appetite for connectivity grew, so did the capabilities of AI. It evolved to not only interpret our data but to predict our behaviors and preferences, cascade content into our feeds that would captivate and engage us, and connect us with brands and causes we care about.

Initial adoptions of AI were modest—simply automating repetitive tasks and handling massive amounts of data more efficiently than a human ever could. This efficiency was invaluable to marketers, content creators, and social media platforms alike, as it freed precious time to focus on creative and strategic endeavors.

The subsequent phase, however, saw not just automation but sophistication and personalization. Machine learning algorithms learned from past interactions to tailor future outcomes. This adaptability meant that every social media user began to experience a uniquely individualized digital environment, which has profound implications for content creators. The content that resonated well was not just well-made, but well-matched to its audience.

Chatbots and virtual assistants became the front-line of customer service, providing instant support and scaling interactions to heights human staff could not reach. They evolved from simple scripted interactions to complex, natural language processing entities that learn and adapt from each conversation.

Content discovery took a leap as AI began to curate and recommend content with uncanny precision. Not only could it match users to content they were likely to enjoy, but it could also help creators and influencers surface their content to those most likely to appreciate it. This refined content dissemination translates into more engagement, retention, and ultimately, conversion.

With the surge in big data, AI became instrumental in sentiment analysis, understanding the mood, opinions, and emotions of the masses. It allowed marketers to capture the zeitgeist of their demographic, reacting to trends and conversations in real-time with unparalleled agility.

Visual recognition technology leapt onto the social scene, changing the way we interact with images and video content. This advancement meant that images, not just textual data, could become a rich source of insights for content optimization and audience engagement strategies.

Then came the predictive analytics that transformed marketing campaigns from reactive to proactive. AI began to forecast user behavior, guiding content creators to not just respond to today's trends but to anticipate tomorrow's. The ability to see ahead and produce content with foresight is no less than a superpower in the competitive world of social media.

AI didn't just evolve in capabilities but also in presence. It's now pervasive, underpinning the operations of every major social media platform. This ubiquity means that there's hardly an aspect of social media that isn't enhanced or influenced by AI, from the content we see to the ads targeted our way.

As we've moved forward, AI integration has become more seamless and less overt, so much so that its presence is felt rather than seen. It underlies sophisticated recommendation engines, influences news feeds, and even plays a role in flagging inappropriate or harmful content, nurturing a safer online community.

Furthermore, the advancement in generative AI has opened new horizons. AI can now not only curate content but also create it. From crafting engaging posts to generating reports, AI's role in content creation has transcended boundaries previously thought insurmountable.

For content creators, understanding the evolution of AI in social media isn't just an academic exercise. It provides a crucial context for leveraging these technologies to their maximum potential. By recognizing where AI has come from, a more informed approach can be integrated into strategies that exploit current trends and prepare for future advancements. Each step of this journey has seen the bar raise higher, the competition fiercer, and the winners more innovative.

The narrative of AI in social media is not one of replacement but of augmentation. AI empowers content creators, taking on the heavy lifting so they can soar, unencumbered by the mundane and free to conjure the extraordinary. It's an invitation to partner with a powerful force to synthesize strategies that resonate, connect, and inspire. AI is the ally that whispers the secrets of an ever-changing social landscape into the ears of those ready to listen.

As we look forward, AI's insatiable march forward promises more disruption, more innovation, and an unending evolution. It's imperative that professionals in the field adapt to these technological winds to stoke the fires of creativity and strategy that propel high-flying campaigns on the currents of progress. The evolution of AI in social media is not just a tale of how we got here but a map that hints at the contours of our digital tomorrow.

The Impact of AI on Social Media Dynamics

Social media's landscape has always been fast-paced and vibrant, with trends surfacing and evaporating at breakneck speeds. Yet, the advent of AI has catalyzed these dynamics, propelling us into an era where technology doesn't just assist; it actively shapes the ebb and flow of online interactions. It's an exhilarating time for marketers, digital strategists, content creators, and professionals – an era where creativity intertwined with AI's analytical prowess can elevate social media endeavors to unprecedented heights.

We're witnessing a seismic shift in social engagement as AI predicts what users want to see, when they want to see it, and in what form. Take, for instance, the seamless personalization feats AI achieves by analyzing copious amounts of data. Individual preferences and behaviors are no longer enigmas, as AI furnishes insights that sculpt a bespoke social media experience for each user. This prescience in delivering content that resonates deeply with users is changing the rules of engagement, compelling content creators to leverage the nuanced understanding AI provides.

Marketing maestros, imagine social ad campaigns that no longer rely on the whims of chance. AI's predictive analytics can dissect past performances, enabling a proactive rather than reactive approach. By mapping out which content electrifies engagement and which fizzles out, AI paves a clear path for creating compelling campaigns that are more likely to captivate and convert.

AI's real-time processing capabilities mean social media is faster and more reactive. Gone are the days of belated trend adoption. AI tools can now identify burgeoning trends with laser precision, allowing content creators to ride the crest of these waves and harness their full potential before they dissipate.

Community management, too, has been revolutionized. AI-driven chatbots, with their near-instant responses and evolving conversation skills, foster a sense of connection and accessibility between brands and audiences. This isn't about replacing the human touch; it's about amplifying it, ensuring that when a human steps in, the conversation is meaningful and rich in context.

From an analytical perspective, AI works tirelessly, distilling oceans of data into actionable insights. Social listening takes on new dimensions, revealing not just what people are talking about, but how they feel about it. Indeed, the sentiment analysis tools AI brings to the table are turning content creators into digital empaths, attuned to the audience's emotions and poised to respond with content that hits the right notes.

AI hasn't just altered how we post on social media; it has transformed content curation. With machine learning algorithms at the helm, content feeds become finely-tuned symphonies of relevance, enhancing user retention and encouraging deeper dives into curated content rabbit holes.

But it's not just about pushing content to the fore; AI ensures that timing is impeccable. With an understanding of global time zones and user activity patterns, AI helps schedule posts for maximum visibility – an orchestration of timing that can ratchet up engagement significantly.

Influencer marketing, a cornerstone of modern social strategy, is also reaping the rewards of AI. Algorithms now assist in identifying influencers whose followers align with a brand's target demographic, optimizing collaborations and ensuring a genuine connection with potential customers.

As AI keeps charting new territory in content relevance, it also presents challenges in creativity. The traditional 'post and pray' method won't slice through the noise. AI requires content creators to elevate their game, combining artistic flair with data-driven insights to craft messages that aren't just seen—they're felt, remembered, and acted upon.

Crisis management has taken a step into the future as well. With AI-driven sentiment analysis and rapid data interpretation, potential issues can be identified and addressed before they snowball into disasters. Reactive strategy has given way to preemptive control, mitigating risks with the foresight that AI affords.

Moreover, AI's introduction to the social realm has birthed new metrics of success. It's no longer just about likes and shares, but also about the depth of interaction and long-term engagement – metrics that AI measures with finesmical precision. Content creators are now empowered to track the lifetime value of a post and understand its ripple effect across the digital sphere.

The integration of AI into social platforms isn't just a back-end novelty—it's an integral part of user-facing features. AI-fueled algorithms are recommending friends, suggesting groups, and even flagging problematic content. But with this power comes a crucial responsibility to ensure these recommendations are fair, unbiased, and ethically sound.

What all of this signals is a transformative period for social media—one of heightened personalization, predictive precision, and analytical acumen. The AI tools at the disposal of today's content creators are not just sophisticated; they're becoming indispensable. Embracing AI's potential allows for a social media presence that's not only more powerful and effective but also more human—more attuned to the very audience it seeks to engage.

As we continue to navigate these dynamic AI-enhanced social media waters, let's acknowledge the profundity of the shift we're experiencing. Content creators, marketers, your craft is no longer just about creating; it's about connecting. And with AI as your compass, the potential to chart new, meaningful territory is boundless. Embrace these changes, harness AI's capabilities, and lean into an era where the confluence of technology and humanity crafts the kind of social media reality that not only reflects but enriches our world.

Chapter 2:
AI and the Content Creator's Journey

Stepping boldly into the world of AI-enhanced creativity means joining forces with a revolutionary ally on your content creation journey. This chapter zeroes in on how artificial intelligence becomes your co-pilot, whispering insights and suggestions, automating the mundane, and injecting a dose of efficiency into your storytelling prowess. As you weave narratives and construct dialogues with your audience, AI tools stand ready to dissect vast seas of data, delivering pearls of wisdom about what resonates with your followers. You'll learn to dance with algorithms that fine-tune your message, ensuring it lands with impact and authenticity. Transcending the traditional, a creator's path is no longer a solitary trek but a synchronized duet with digital intuition, amplifying the reach and touching the hearts of those who consume your crafted content. Dive into this chapter to uncover how embracing the essentials of AI can elevate your creative narrative and transform your digital odyssey into an epic tale of connection and engagement.

The Essentials of AI-Enabled Content Creation

Embark upon the journey of AI-enabled content creation with a discerning eye, willing to unravel intricacies and potentialities tucked within this tech-laden realm. AI isn't merely a tool; it represents a paradigm shift, enveloping the content creation landscape. Herein lies the key to unlocking a trove of opportunities that can elevate social media presence to unprecedented heights. Equipped with artificial intelligence, the quintessential content creator transforms into a maestro, orchestrating a symphony of engagement and innovation.

Understanding the strengths of AI is pivotal. Picture artificial intelligence as a cog in the machine that never tires, a silent partner that pores over vast datasets with ease, spotting trends invisible to the human eye. This partner can generate ideas at breakneck speed, tailor content with precision, and carry out tasks with a spectrum of complexity. Yet, it remains a tool, albeit advanced, that requires human oversight to wield its capabilities effectively.

How, then, does one meld creativity with efficiency, intuition with analytics? Start by framing AI as the ultimate enhancer. It is the crucible for refining content strategy, for AI discerns which topics sizzle and which fizzle amongst audiences. It gauges sentiment with aplomb and predicts content affinity with compelling accuracy. The marriage of these insights with human ingenuity is where true content magic is born.

Embrace AI for what it is—a canvas stretcher, not the painter. It stretches the canvas of possibility so that creators can paint with broader, more vivid strokes. By using AI-assisted tools, one can craft more relevant and compelling narratives. Its ability to augment linguistic patterns enables the creation of engaging and relatable material that resonates on a personal level with the target audience.

In the intricate dance of content creation, rhythm is established through the consistency and timing of posts. AI's analytical prowess steps in here, recommending optimal posting schedules based on user activity and engagement patterns. The creator's intuition, balanced with data-driven insights, results in a posting cadence that hits the right notes at the right times.

However, it's not only about pushing out content; it's about sparking conversations. AI's role in understanding audience responses, shaping follow-up content, and engagement strategies is invaluable. A creator's wit, coupled with AI's assessment of trending topics and sentiment analysis, can sculpt conversations that are not just relevant but also deeply engaging.

Yet, with great power comes great responsibility. A content creator's authentic voice must never be drowned by AI's capabilities. It's critical to keep the human element front and center. Content must embody the brand's values and message while leveraging AI to amplify reach and relevance.

Additionally, AI can democratize content creation. It liberates creators from the mundane, automating repetitive tasks, and empowering them to focus on the artistry that machines cannot replicate. In turn, this symbiosis drives productivity, enriching the creative process rather than stifling it.

Still, one must tread wisely. Though AI can generate content, it should be harnessed to suggest ideas and provide a framework rather than generate an entire narrative. The human touch must embellish the skeletal structure that AI provides, ensuring that the content feels authentic and personal.

Equally important is the understanding that AI is not infallible. It operates within the confines of its programming and the data it is fed. Thus, a mindful content creator must regularly audit and fine-tune their AI tools to mitigate biases and inaccuracies that can inevitably seep in.

Venturing into AI-enabled content creation also demands a level of agility and resilience. Algorithms evolve, platforms update, and audience preferences shift. The content creator must be as adaptive as the AI itself, learning and relearning, experimenting and iterating, maintaining a growth mindset that thrives amidst change.

As you wield AI, let it not overshadow the essence of your brand's story. Use AI as a companion in your creative odyssey, letting it guide you to the stars but never piloting the ship itself. Remember that in the realm of social media, authenticity and relatability are your most valuable assets. AI, when harnessed with discernment, simply becomes a means to enhance those qualities.

In sum, the essentials of AI-enabled content creation are a blend of understanding, creativity, responsibility, and constant evolution. Embrace AI not as a replacement but as an extension of your creative toolkit—a remarkable asset that, when used wisely, can transform the content landscape. Strive to leverage this powerful technology to forge deeper connections, innovate relentlessly, and tell captivating stories that enthrall and inspire.

As this nexus of human creativity and artificial intelligence grows ever more intertwined, there lies a promise of boundless horizons. It's time for creators to dive deep into the essentials of AI-enabled content creation and emerge as pioneers shaping the future of the digital storytelling paradigm.

Navigating the AI Content Creation Landscape

In the vibrant terrain of AI-assisted creation, it's easy to feel like you're traipsing through an uncharted wilderness. The horizon is dotted with a bewildering array of tools, each promising to catapult your content to the stratosphere of engagement and visibility. Here, amidst the digital flora and fauna, the modern content creator must find their path.

First and foremost, understanding the terrain is vital. AI content creation isn't a monolith; it's a kaleidoscope of capabilities ranging from text generation to predictive analytics, from image creation to video editing enhancements. Each tool serves a unique purpose and mastering the art lies in knowing when and how to use them.

Navigating this landscape means adopting a mindset of exploration. Just as early pathfinders relied on compass and sextant, so too must creators lean into analytics and feedback loops. These instruments help steer your content strategy in response to the ever-shifting demands of audience preferences and platform algorithms.

The savvy explorer doesn't set forth without a map. The map, in our case, translates to a deep dive into the audience's psyche. AI tools furnish insights that cut through guesswork; they illuminate demographic quirks, engagement patterns, and content preferences that one might otherwise overlook.

Adaptation isn't just a concept; it's your new best friend. The digital ecosystem is dynamic, and survival often means pivoting with agility. AI offers the ability to quickly realign content strategies based on real-time data, ensuring your output remains relevant and resonant.

Understanding the array of tools at your disposal is critical. It's not enough to know of them; mastery comes from understanding their nuances - the strengths, weaknesses, and the scenarios in which they shine. Whether it's a language model that can mimic your brand's tone or a design tool that aligns with your visual identity, the right AI leverages can elevate your content from good to great.

Don't fall for the siren call of over-automation. AI augments, not replaces, the human touch in creativity. Content that connects is born of empathy and emotion, something that AI is still chasing the tail winds of. Integrating AI should enhance your creativity, not stifle it - fostering a collaborative dance between human intuition and machine efficiency.

As with any journey, there will be trials. Not every AI experiment will yield gold. Some will falter, a few may even fail spectacularly. But it's through these iterations that you'll uncover the potent blend of AI and human creativity that defines your brand's voice in the digital chorus.

Safeguard your authenticity, for it is the banner under which your content will march. Amidst the clamor of AI-generated content, originality stands out. Use AI to amplify what's uniquely yours - your perspective, your voice, your story. This is the compass that guides through the noise, the beacon that brings your audience home.

An oft-overlooked aspect is ethics in the age of AI. As you journey through this terrain, remember the importance of transparency. With great power comes great responsibility, and it's crucial to disclose AI's role in your content creation process. Trust is the currency of the realm, and it's won through honesty and integrity.

Managing the deluge of possibilities requires a filter - a set of criteria against which to measure each new tool or tactic. Does it serve your brand's purpose? Does it resonate with your audience? Does it adhere to the ethical standards you uphold? These questions are the sieves that separate the wheat from the chaff.

Expanding your toolkit means embracing continuous learning. The AI landscape is in constant flux, teeming with innovation and evolution. Dedicating time to stay abreast of the latest developments is not just recommended; it's essential to maintain the relevance and efficacy of your content strategies.

Remember that the journey of AI engagement is iterative. Every piece of content is a stepping stone towards deeper understanding and finesse. Build on the analytics and insights provided by AI to fine-tune your messaging, timing, and delivery. It's in this incremental progression that proficiency is honed.

You're not alone on this trek. Communities of fellow creators are navigating the same wilds, encountering similar challenges, sharing insights, and strategies. Engage with these communities to exchange knowledge, and perhaps even forge partnerships that can amplify your reach and impact.

In conclusion, navigating the AI content creation landscape is not for the faint of heart. It calls for curiosity, adaptability, and a pioneering spirit. But for those willing to embrace the journey, the rewards are manifold - a rich, dynamic, and ultimately more impactful content creation process. Thus, your odyssey in the AI-infused expanse of content creation is not just about surviving; it's about thriving in an exhilarating confluence of technology and creativity.

Chapter 3:
Crafting Your AI Social Media Strategy

As we turn the digital page from understanding the broad impacts of AI on content creation, it's time to roll up your sleeves and sketch out a detailed blueprint that instills AI at the heart of your social media strategy. When venturing into this terrain, you must be as precise as an artisan, yet as creative as an artist. Setting achievable goals is the cornerstone of this process; it's about defining what success looks like when AI enriches your campaigns, ensuring that your ambitions are in lockstep with technological capabilities. The synthesis of AI into your social media plan should be seamless, harmonizing with existing human-driven efforts and enhancing them rather than replacing. The orchestration of strategies that leverage this intelligent technology will be your compass in the vast sea of digital interaction. This chapter is where strategic foresight meets practical action—where you'll tailor a social media strategy augmented by AI, one that not only reaches but also resonates with your audience, pushing the envelope of what's possible in this dynamically connected world.

Setting Achievable Goals with AI

In the quest to infuse AI into your social media strategy, the crux lies in setting attainable targets that echo the potent capabilities of AI while staying grounded in realism. Imagine AI as a compass, guiding your brand through the vast ocean of online interactions, arming you with insights and automation that make lofty goals feel within reach. By articulating clear, measurable objectives, you'll harness the precision of algorithms to carve out a path toward data-driven success. Think incrementally—what can AI achieve for you this quarter, or in this particular campaign? Whether it's increasing engagement rates, amplifying reach, or sharpening the precision of targeted marketing, align AI's robust analytics and pattern-detection with goals that will elevate your brand's digital presence. This fusion of cutting-edge tech and strategic finesse will not only set a high bar but also chart a course to victory that is as innovative as it is achievable.

Defining Success in AI-Augmented Campaigns

When it comes to wielding the formidable power of artificial intelligence in your social media campaigns, defining what success looks like is crucial. Success, in this arena, isn't a one-size-fits-all scenario. It's as varied as the creators behind the campaigns and the audiences they serve. So how do we chart a course through this complex landscape and claim victory?

Imagine this: you've set sail on the vast ocean of digital marketing with AI as your compass. You've got an arsenal of tools at your disposal, with data and algorithms ready to guide you. But without a destination in mind—a definition of what success means to you—even the most sophisticated technology can't save you from drifting aimlessly.

Success in AI-augmented campaigns can be measured by a myriad of metrics, but it's essential to focus on those which align with your strategic goals. Are you looking to drive engagement, boost sales, or increase brand awareness? Perhaps you're aiming to enhance customer satisfaction or automate tasks to free up creative time. Pinpointing your primary objective will act as your North Star, guiding your use of AI towards a victorious outcome.

In the context of social media content creation, success often translates to a blend of quantitative and qualitative metrics. The numbers tell a story—follower counts, engagement rates, click-throughs—

painting a picture of popularity and reach. Yet, the quality of interactions, sentiment analysis, and the richness of user-generated content can often speak louder than statistics alone.

But let's break it down even further. In the AI-augmented world, success means harnessing no mere hodgepodge of features and functions; it's about integration and cohesion. AI should amplify your content's relevance, ensuring it reaches the right eyes at the ideal moment. Through predictive analysis, AI can forecast when your audience is most active and receptive, lifting your engagement rates skyward.

Success also means personalization. With AI, every interaction can be tailored, making each follower feel like the hero of their own story, which is told with your brand as a central theme. By feeding AI the correct data, you can transform customer experiences from generic to genuinely personal, fostering a deeper connection between your audience and your brand.

And let's not forget about creativity. It might seem counterintuitive, but AI can liberate your creativity. With mundane tasks automated, success takes the form of newfound time and space for innovation. Your human ingenuity, unshackled from the tedium of content scheduling and data analysis, can now craft stories that captivate and inspire.

Efficiency is yet another hallmark of success. AI is the swift wind in your sails, propelling you towards your objectives with greater speed. Machine learning algorithms can optimize your campaigns in real-time, identifying and adapting to trends faster than any human could. Success, in this sense, is a more streamlined, responsive campaign that can pivot with the ever-changing tides of the digital world.

However, AI-augmented success isn't solely about the immediate impact; it's about sustainability. In the dynamic seas of social media, what works today may sink tomorrow. So, long-term success involves

AI's ability to learn and evolve, ensuring your campaigns remain buoyant through constant optimization and learning from past performances. This kind of success breeds campaigns that are not just flashes in the pan but enduring beacons of your brand's prowess.

Importantly, success in AI-augmented campaigns is reflected in ROI. The ultimate barometer for any business activity, return on investment here means that every dollar spent on AI tools and tech yields substantial returns, be it through direct sales, lead generation, or the incremental value of brand equity.

The essence of success in AI-powered campaigns is also in its transparency and trackability. With a multitude of data points to consider, AI allows for an unprecedented level of analysis. You're no longer shooting in the dark; you're making data-backed decisions that illuminate the path to success.

It's vital, too, to recognize that success with AI demands responsible use. As you leverage this powerful tech, maintaining ethical standards and respecting user privacy remains paramount. The triumph of any campaign also lies in the trust and goodwill it fosters among its audience. So, success is also about deploying AI in a way that's conscious of its footprint in peoples' lives and society at large.

In the orchestra of AI-augmented campaigns, every instrument must play its part. Content creators are the conductors, guiding the symphony to a crescendo. Success, therefore, is the harmony between man and machine, creating a melody that resonates across the digital soundscape—a tune that lingers in the minds of its listeners long after the last note has played.

Finally, defining success in your AI-augmented campaigns is about vision and adaptability. It's a dynamic process where you set clear, measurable objectives and remain agile enough to change course when the data reveals new opportunities. It's about crafting content and experiences that not only engage and convert but also endure.

So, as you steer your ship through the bustling waters of social media, let AI be your steadfast crewmember, your navigator, and occasionally, your first mate. With clear definition and unwavering pursuit of these varied facets of success, your journey is bound to be not only prosperous but also pioneering in the realm of digital interaction and content creation.

Integrating AI into Your Overall Social Media Plan

In the swiftly evolving landscape of social media, artificial intelligence (AI) is not just an asset; it's a game changer. Embedding AI into your social media plan requires a strategic approach that harmonizes with your broader digital objectives. Gone are the days of piecemeal implementation. For a transformative impact, AI must be intricately woven into the very fabric of your social media strategy.

To start, identify the aspects of your social media activities that can benefit the most from AI. Whether it's content creation, customer service, user engagement, or analytics, AI can provide leverage. However, the secret sauce lies in understanding that AI is better at enhancing human creativity and efficiency rather than replacing it. It supplements your unique perspective with unprecedented scalability and insights.

With goals established, incorporate AI in a way that prioritizes these objectives. Be it increasing audience engagement or driving more traffic to your website, align AI tools towards these ends. Ensure that the tools chosen align with the particular nuances of the respective platforms you use, may it be Twitter's real-time conversations or Instagram's visual storytelling.

As AI integration proceeds, maintain a culture of testing and learning. The virtual landscape is a testing ground where AI's algorithms learn from every interaction and piece of content. By experimenting with different AI-driven content types and messages, you will find the combination that best resonates with your target audience. Here, the motto is progress over perfection; allow room for growth and refinement.

Don't limit the role of AI to just posting times or content creation; let it dive deep into predictive analytics. AI's ability to analyze vast troves of data will help you understand not only when your audience is online but also predict future trends. This forward-looking analysis should inform your content calendar, making it dynamic and ever-responsive to audience needs.

While embarking on automated conversations with chatbots, be cautious. The blend of AI-driven chatbots should be seamless, offering assistance and engagement while maintaining brand voice. AI should feel like a natural continuation of your brand's interaction with the audience, not a robotic interruption.

As content is disseminated, use AI to monitor real-time responses and adapt strategies accordingly. The agility that AI offers should embolden you to pivot quickly in response to user behavior, seizing opportunities as they emerge, and retreating from less effective tactics.

In the domain of customer insights, AI is inarguably potent. Delving into the psychographics of your audience, AI can unearth patterns and preferences that are invisible to the naked eye. These insights can drive not just your content strategy but can also inform product development and marketing strategies.

Also, keep humanity at the forefront when leveraging AI for personalization. The aim is to make each user feel understood and valued on an individual level, not to overwhelm or cross the fine line of privacy. Calibrate AI to enhance user experience by suggesting relevant content, rather than being intrusive.

While you navigate the possibilities of AI in social media, maintain a rigorous approach toward measuring the success of AI-integrated strategies. Employ AI tools that track vital metrics and KPIs, ensuring that you stay focused on outcomes that propel your brand forward.

Amidst all the integration, it's critical to stay alert to the ever-evolving AI landscape. The tools that are cutting-edge today may be obsolete tomorrow. Remain responsive to changes in technology, continuously scouting for new ways AI can enhance your overall plan.

Even as you scale heights with AI, ground your strategy in ethical practices. The expanding capabilities of AI must be matched by a deepened commitment to responsible usage, ensuring that AI acts in service to human values and brand integrity.

Lastly, foster a team culture that embraces AI and its potential. Educate and empower your social media managers, content creators, and strategists to utilize AI tools effectively. Encourage them to envision AI as a collaborator that amplifies their creativity, not a competitor that usurps their role.

Integration of AI into your overall social media strategy is an ongoing journey. It requires a visionary mindset, a willingness to experiment, and a commitment to iterative learning. But the rewards – enhanced engagement, deeper insights, improved efficiency, and a sharper competitive edge – signal a revolution in the way social media serves to connect us all.

Remember, the symphony of AI in your social media plan is not about automating the art of human connection but rather, it's about augmenting the capabilities that allow us to understand and interact with our audience in ways that were inconceivable in the pre-AI era. Move forward with intention, understanding that each step you take with AI brings you closer not only to your business goals but to forging deeper, more meaningful connections with your audience.

Chapter 4:
AI Tools for Enhanced
Content Creation

As we transition from the conceptual frameworks outlined in the previous chapters, let's immerse ourselves in the tangible assets that will revolutionize your content: AI tools. These digital craftsmen wield algorithms like fine brushes, crafting messages with an intricacy and precision that human hands can't always match. Imagine wielding a suite of tools that not only streamline content production but infuse it with a level of creativity and personalization previously unattainable. From natural language generation software transforming dry data into captivating narratives to AI-driven design tools that customize visuals to the user's taste, we're entering a realm where the quintessence of your brand can be communicated with unprecedented consistency and flair. Guiding you through the labyrinthine array of options, this chapter leans into the art of selecting the AI companions that align with your unique storytelling needs, ensuring that each piece of content not only reaches its target audience but resonates with them on a deeper level. Embrace these instruments of innovation, and let them amplify your creative potential, enabling you to craft messages that soar through the digital noise and into the hearts and minds of your audience.

Identifying the Right AI Tools for Your Needs

In the quest for digital mastery, settling on the correct set of AI tools for content creation is not merely a luxury—it's a necessity. With the myriad of solutions out there, how does one navigate this bustling techscape and pinpoint tools that not only align with your strategic goals but also amplify your creative potential? Let's dive into the how-tos of identifying the right AI tools that can transform your social media content from good to great.

What's vital to realize is that there's no one-size-fits-all when it comes to AI tool selection. The initial step is introspective – you need to analyze your specific content creation needs thoroughly. Are you looking to generate text-based content, enhance visuals, or perhaps both? Understanding your ultimate goal, whether it's to increase engagement, boost productivity, or enhance creativity, is the first marker on the road map to decision-making.

Consider what the core of your strategy is. For instance, if data-driven insights are what you're after, then AI tools that excel in analytics would be your go-to companions. Look for platforms that offer deep learning algorithms capable of dissecting audience behavior and preference patterns. This type of tool will enable you to make informed decisions that ensure your content resonates with your target audience.

Undeniably, integration is key in a world where time is a non-renewable resource. Seek out tools that blend seamlessly with your existing workflows. You need AI solutions that can synchronize with your current software ecosystems, cutting down on the time spent in task-switching and the potential pain of adopting new tacit knowledge.

Quality content creation is as much an art as it is a science. Thus, lean towards AI tools that nurture your brand's voice and tone. The technology should be sophisticated enough to discern nuances in language, style, and sentiment, producing content that's not just accurate but eloquently tailored to your brand's persona.

The paramount aspect of budget cannot be understated. Investing in AI should not break the bank but rather be a strategic allocation of resources that promises a healthy return. Explore pricing models of various tools and gauge the cost against the value it pledges to bring. Sometimes, a subscription-based model works best; other times, a one-time purchase makes more fiscal sense.

Ease of use is another non-negotiable attribute. The learning curve associated with a new tool can often be steep and treacherous. Opt for AI solutions that boast user-friendly interfaces and provide robust support and training resources.

An aspect that's often overlooked is scalability. Your chosen AI tool should not just serve your current needs but also have the capability to grow with you. As your brand evolves and your audience expands, the tool should adapt accordingly, without the need to start the selection process anew.

Security considerations should also be at the forefront. In this data-centric age, ensure the AI tool you choose is compliant with privacy laws and industry standards. Safeguarding your and your clients' data is not just about integrity; it's about maintaining trust and upholding your brand's reputation.

Don't forget about the community and support around an AI tool. Digital tools don't exist in a vacuum—they thrive in ecosystems where ideas are shared, and issues are resolved collectively. Favor AI tools that have active user communities and accessible customer support.

Creativity in AI tool selection also means keeping an eye out for versatility. The optimal tool isn't a one-trick pony but rather one that offers a suite of features. Such versatility ensures that your workflow remains integrated, and your creative output is diversified.

Let's also talk about feedback mechanisms. The ability for an AI tool to learn from its outputs and user interactions is indispensable. Look for platforms that incorporate user feedback into their algorithms, continuously refining the quality of the content produced.

In the end, an AI tool is as good as the results it delivers. Before committing to a platform, trial periods can be incredibly revealing. They offer a firsthand experience of what working with the AI will be like and whether it meets the expectations set by its own marketing.

Lastly, remember that success in the digital realm is often about agility and readiness to adapt. Aim for AI tools that are constantly updated and improved upon, matching the pace at which social media evolves.

Armed with these pointers, you're well on your way to unlocking the potential of AI in your content creation process. The right tool isn't just a silent partner—it's an engine for innovation, a medium for expression, and a catalyst for growth.

Best Practices for AI Tool Adoption and Usage

Entering the world of AI-enhanced content creation is not just about selecting the right tools; it's about weaving these technologies into the very fabric of your content strategy—a process both thrilling and complex. Cutting-edge as it may be, the adoption of AI tools comes with a learning curve that demands patience and strategic foresight. A visionary content creator doesn't simply ride the wave of innovation; they harness its power to fuel a transformative journey.

The first step towards adopting AI tools is to approach them with a mindset that's receptive to experimentation. Remember, AI is not a magic wand, but a powerful ally that can amplify your creative potential. Begin with a pilot project, something small-scale that allows you to tinker with the AI tool of your choice. This approach allows you to build familiarity with the tool's capabilities and quirks in a controlled environment.

Once you've dipped your toes in the water, it's vital to set clear objectives. What do you hope to achieve with AI? Whether it's enhancing the quality of your content, increasing engagement, or driving sales, your goals should align with the strengths of AI. Keep these goals SMART—Specific, Measurable, Achievable, Relevant, and Timebound. This clarity acts as your north star, guiding your AI tool usage.

Integration doesn't happen overnight. It's a step-by-step process that should be methodical. Begin by integrating AI into one aspect of your content creation process at a time. Whether it's idea generation, content curation, or audience analysis, starting with a single facet helps prevent overwhelm and clears the path for a smoother transition.

Documentation is your friend. As you integrate AI into your workflow, meticulously record your processes, observations, and results. Such records are invaluable; they're reference points that help you identify patterns, successes, and areas needing refinement. They're tangible evidence of your journey that informs your future decisions.

Knowledge sharing is also crucial within your team. Collaborate, discuss, and disseminate information about the AI tools you're using. Synthesize your collective insights to foster an environment where AI tools aren't just individual gadgets but a communal treasury of resources that liven up your collective creative spirit.

Another important best practice is choosing scalability. The AI tools you select should accommodate anticipated growth, not just meet present needs. In a fast-paced digital landscape, your tools must be agile, scaling up as your brand and strategy evolve. Look for AI solutions that promise adaptability and longevity.

As you navigate the integration of AI tools into your content creation process, data security and privacy should never be an afterthought. Ensure you're using tools compliant with industry standards and legislation. Your audience's trust is a cornerstone of your digital reputation and must be guarded with the utmost diligence.

Let analytics be the compass that guides your AI tool usage. AI-fueled insights can pave the way for nuanced understanding and actionable intelligence. It's not just about collecting data; it's about translating it into strategies that captivate and resonate with your target audience.

Customization is also essential. While off-the-shelf AI tools are convenient, tailoring them to fit your unique voice and brand is what elevates your content. Customization can be the difference between content that feels generic and content that pulsates with the distinct heartbeat of your brand's ethos.

Tapping into user feedback is a powerful way to ensure your AI tools are serving their purpose. Encourage your audience to provide feedback on the content facilitated by AI. This feedback becomes a rich soil out of which can grow improved content strategies, more attuned to the desires of your audience.

Moreover, remain aware of the need for human touch. AI excels at processing data and generating efficient outputs, but the nuances of human emotion and storytelling prowess are irreplaceable. Balance AI's analytical prowess with the warmth of human creativity. This synergy creates content that resonates on a human level.

Avoid becoming overly reliant on AI. The most effective content creators use AI as an extension of their capabilities, not as a crutch. Strive for a harmonious dance between AI-driven efficiency and human-driven intuition. This balance preserves the authenticity that fosters genuine connections with your audience.

Through it all, prioritize ongoing education. The landscape of AI is continually shifting, and keeping abreast of the latest trends, tools, and techniques is paramount. Engage with online courses, webinars, and other resources to keep sharpening your skills. This appetite for knowledge positions you as a forward-thinking creator in the AI landscape.

Finally, embrace the iterative nature of working with AI. This approach fosters a culture of perpetual refinement and adaptation. Each piece of content created, each campaign launched, can be viewed as a draft, ever-evolving towards a greater emblem of your brand's evolving story. As you masterfully wield the tools of AI, let them be the brush with which you paint the canvas of digital engagement, ever striving for that compelling masterpiece that captures the gaze of a world in constant motion.

Chapter 5:
Personalization and AI:
The Power Duo

In a world where every click, like, and share are fragments of the digital identity puzzle, Personalization and AI have emerged as the undeniable champions in the art of digital marketing finesse. This transformative pairing goes beyond merely addressing consumers by their first names; it delves deep into the catacombs of data, sieves through the mundane, and emerges with golden nuggets of user-specific insights that can catapult engagement rates into the stratosphere. This chapter is a treasure map for content creators who yearn to craft messages that stick, campaigns that resonate, and branding that feels as intimate as a heart-to-heart chat. By combining the latest AI algorithms with a deep understanding of audience behaviors and preferences, the modern marketer isn't just shouting into the void—they're whispering into the ears of an audience who feels seen, heard, and valued. This isn't just marketing; this is the convergence of technology and human desire, an elegant dance between numbers and emotions, a strategy where every piece of content is a chameleon, adapting to fit the unique colorings of individual perspectives and contexts.

Leveraging AI for Hyper-Personalization

Step into the realm of hyper-personalization—with the precision of a maestro and the insight of a soothsayer, AI is reshaping the landscape of tailored social media content. Envision a world where each piece of content strikes a chord with individual audience members, engaging them at an unprecedented personal level. AI's capacity to deep dive into data lakes yields rich insights into user preferences, behaviors, and triggers. These insights not only fuel the creation of content that resonates on a near-spiritual level but also drive real-time adaptation to consumer micro-movements. Far beyond static customer segments, AI tailors the experience to an audience of one, dynamically creating that 'just for me' sensation. It's the careful orchestration of this data that cultivates a fertile ground for brands to grow loyalty and conversion, pinpointing and responding to the ever-evolving tapestry of human desire.

Creating Content That Resonates: AI Insights and Analytics

In the buzzing world of social media, content is king, but relevance is the kingdom. As storytellers, influencers, and brand stewards, the onus falls upon you to spin yarns that capture hearts, turn heads, and inspire action. This quest for resonant content can often feel like a minefield. Fear not, for these are not insurmountable woes. When AI's insights and analytics enter the stage, content creators are bestowed with a sort of divining rod for resonance.

Picture this: a landscape rich with data, where every like, share, and comment is a pixel in a larger picture of your audience's desires and demands. Artificial Intelligence, your steadfast companion, sifts through this digital mosaic, extracting patterns and preferences with a finesse no human could match in ten lifetimes. The insights it illuminates are not mere numbers; they are the stardust that, when sprinkled upon your content, makes it shine with relevance.

How, you might ask, does one harness this power? It begins with an understanding that resonance is not stumbled upon by accident. It's engineered. AI analytics tools are the architects of this engineering, transforming your content from a static monologue into a dynamic dialogue. They track the zeitgeist of your audience's behavior, illuminating what content performs best and why. With these insights, you're no longer shooting arrows in the dark but rather, targeting with precision the bullseye of audience engagement.

Take sentiment analysis, a jewel in the crown of AI analytics. It reads the emotional undercurrents of online conversations, providing a more nuanced understanding of how your content makes people feel. Does your latest post incite joy, provoke thought, or inspire trust? AI knows, and it can guide you like a compass to the true north of audience connection.

But the wizardry doesn't stop there. Imagine having the ability to predict the impact of your content before it even kisses the digital ether. Predictive analytics stoke the fires of foresight, allowing you to anticipate trends and ride the wave rather than chase it. Such tools peer through the mist of uncertainty and draw a map towards content that not only resonates but captivates, becoming a conversation piece and not just a fleeting impression.

Content segmentation, though less glamorous, is equally important. It is the art of dividing your audience into subgroups, ensuring that your message reaches the most receptive ears. No longer must you appeal to the masses with broad strokes; AI helps tailor your message to resonate with specific segments, making each post a masterstroke of relevance.

Yet, with great power comes great responsibility. The ethical dimension of AI analytics can't be overstressed. When used responsibly, AI is not a tool for manipulation but rather for empathetic connection. It helps you speak to people in the language they understand and appreciate, acknowledging their unique perspectives and values.

While data-driven insights are paramount, the soul of your content remains in the human touch. AI should augment creativity, not supplant it. The narratives, stories, and emotions that blossom in your content are your domain; AI's role is to nurture and feed them with the waters of insight so they can grow strong and vibrant.

In the pursuit of resonant content, continuity is key. AI's analytics roll out the thread on which the pearls of your content are strung, ensuring consistency with your brand voice and ethos. Brand consistency is the steady drumbeat to which your audience's hearts synchronize; dissonance is the thief of resonance.

Speaking of continuity, A/B testing offers a pathway to perpetual improvement. It's the crucible in which your content is refined. By serving different variations of your posts and measuring the outcomes, AI-driven A/B testing reveals what elements resonate most profoundly. This iterative process is a dance with data, leading to content that is ever more resonant, relevant, and effective.

The granular analytics provided by AI offer a window into content engagement at a micro-level. Understanding which parts of your videos are rewatched, what paragraphs in your articles retain readers, and what images in your posts garner the most attention—these insights are invaluable. They are the compass bearings guiding the tiny adjustments that cumulatively lift your content from good to exceptional.

Let's not overlook the behemoth of video content, which reigns supreme in the online kingdom. AI's video analytics break down watch times, drop-off points, and engagement peaks to paint a vivid picture of viewer behavior. In the land of the scrolling thumb, keeping a viewer's attention is akin to catching lightning in a bottle. With AI's insights, that elusive electricity is not just captured—it's harnessed.

With these AI-powered tools at your disposal, the elusive art of creating resonant content feels less like alchemy and more like science. Yet, do remember, data is not the painter but the palette. It's the range of colors from which you, the artist, choose to create your masterpiece.

It's the silence between the notes that makes the music. You are the maestro orchestrating the symphony, with AI serving as your finest instrument.

Don't shy away from the power of AI insights and analytics, for they are your torch in a cave of possibilities, illuminating the hidden passages to your audience's heart. Equipped with these AI companions by your side, there's no telling the heights your content can reach. It's not merely about being louder in the cacophony of the digital arena, but about striking the right chord that echoes through the noise.

Last but not least, do remember that the canvas of digital content is ever-expanding. As you wield AI's insights and analytics with finesse, let yourself be immersed in the possibilities. Let every post you craft be a bridge, every campaign a journey, every storyboard a launchpad into the hearts and minds of those you seek to move. In this convergence of data and creativity, lies your path to content that doesn't just resonate—it reverberates across the expansive universe of digital engagement.

Chapter 6:
Harnessing AI for Content Distribution

As we pivot from the intricacies of AI-powered personalization, it becomes evident that the true prowess of a well-oiled content machine lies in its ability to place the right content in front of the right eyes at the right time. In this chapter, we delve into the realm where artificial intelligence transforms from a creator's companion into a savvy distributor, masterminding the dissemination of your content across the vast social media landscape. We'll explore how AI isn't just reshaping content creation but is also revolutionizing distribution through automated scheduling and predictive analysis, ensuring each post strikes a chord when the audience is most receptive. By tapping into algorithms that learn from countless data points, AI equips you with a crystal ball, offering foresight into peak engagement times and content preferences. It's a game where anticipation meets precision, and our goal is to harness this symbiotic relationship between technological advancement and human creativity to captivate and grow our digital tribes. So let's unpack how you can command these intelligent systems to echo your brand's voice across the digital expanse, turning the unpredictable art of content dissemination into a science of strategic triumph.

Automated Scheduling and AI Predictive Analysis

Embracing the future of content distribution means more than just crafting stunning posts; it's about ensuring those digital masterpieces hit the social waves at the prime moment for impact. Automated scheduling harnesses the precision of AI to catapult your content into the timelines of your audience when they're most receptive. But the magic doesn't stop at timing. AI predictive analysis delves into the mosaic of online behavior, extracting patterns and preferences that are invisible to the naked eye. This potent combination empowers you to anticipate which content will sizzle and which will fizzle, before you even press "Publish." With this foresight, you're not just riding the wave—you're steering it, paving the way for engagement rates that defy gravity and a presence that lingers in the mind long after the screen fades to black.

Timing is Everything: Optimizing Post Schedules with AI

In the intricate ballet of social media, timing can make or break the connection between your content and your audience. In the endlessly cascading stream of digital communication, ensuring your content reaches its intended viewers at the right moment is not just desirable – it's imperative. Just as a seasoned conductor intuitively knows how to align the orchestra for an impactful crescendo, so must the content creator master the rhythms of audience engagement. Here, the conductor's baton is wielded not just by human intuition but enhanced by the precision of artificial intelligence.

In this era where information never sleeps, the adept content creator must ascertain not only what to say but when to say it. The audience's online presence fluctuates, peaking at certain hours and waning in others. Artificial Intelligence (AI) helps navigate these digital waters, analyzing dense data to predict optimal posting times. With AI at your side, you can discern patterns that are invisible to the naked eye, patterns sculpted by time zones, by work schedules, by life's unpredictable ebb and flow.

Imagine a tool so adept at learning from your past content success-es and failures that it can forecast the future. That's what AI brings to the table. By gleaning insights from vast datasets including engagement rates, shares, and even the type of content consumed, AI becomes an oracle of post scheduling. Effective AI tools analyze these data points, comparing them against broader social media usage trends to suggest the best times to post for each specific platform.

It's crucial to grasp that this isn't a one-time analysis. The digital landscape is as mutable as the sea. Trends shift, algorithms evolve, and audience behaviors transform. AI is not static; it constantly learns, im-proving its predictive capabilities over time. The more you use AI to optimize your posting schedule, the more accurate it becomes. This iterative effect is one of the cornerstones of AI's value in social media strategy.

The intelligent orchestration of content does not end with know-ing 'when'; the 'what' and 'how' are equally pivotal. AI tools can tie the knots between different types of content and the best times for their deployment. For example, video content may engage users more effectively during evening hours when they are free to consume longer formats, while quick, snappy updates may perform better during the midday slump when users are scrolling for a brief escape.

There's a layer of customization in AI's capabilities that is critical to understand. Your audience is unique, and your AI's learning needs to be aligned with your brand's specific followers. Seasoned marketers know that while generalized best-time-to-post guides offer a starting point, true optimization comes from an intimate understanding of your own audience's habits.

Aligning post schedules with audience preferences also implies an understanding of different time zones. Brands with a global reach need to think beyond the confines of their local timing. AI helps in segment-ing audiences geographically, ensuring your content reaches users when they are most likely to be attentive, regardless of where they are in the world.

Moreover, this sophistication extends to the type of AI you choose. There are myriad options out there, each with different strengths. Some may offer basic insights based on existing metrics, while others bring more advanced predictive analytics to bear, considering factors such as seasonal variations, current events, and even competitor activities.

In deploying AI to define your posting schedule, also consider the multiplicity of platforms. Each social media channel has unique characteristics and user behaviors. AI tools that specialize in cross-platform analysis will give you a holistic view, tailoring your content rhythm to each channel's unique beat.

Understand that adopting AI for scheduling is not about supplanting human insight but augmenting it. The powerful combination of human creativity and AI's analytical prowess can push your social media strategy beyond conventional boundaries. You're not merely posting; you're strategically placing content where and when it has the greatest potential to thrive.

Privacy and data usage concerns also intertwine with AI scheduling tools. Ethical use of data is paramount, and so is compliance with regulations such as GDPR. AI tools must be transparent and responsible in their data handling, ensuring that optimization does not come at the cost of user privacy.

As with any tool, one must not become overly reliant on AI scheduling without understanding its logic. Blind faith can lead to missed opportunities or even missteps. Take time to interpret the AI recommendations and use them as informed suggestions rather than hard and fast rules. Know that AI is your partner in this dance, not the lead that you follow without question.

Implementing AI for optimizing post schedules also means you're committing to a constantly evolving strategy. Monitor the results not just for the uptick in likes or shares but for the deeper story they tell about your audience's changing behaviors and preferences. Let the data guide your path, adjusting as the landscape of digital engagement changes.

To round out your AI-augmented scheduling strategy, remember to stay agile. If an unexpected event occurs, you must be ready to pivot, even if AI tells you it's the perfect time to post. Your audience will appreciate the human element behind your brand - that you're in tune not just with data, but with the context of the world around them.

So, as you chart your course through the dynamic waters of content creation, let AI navigate the tides of timing. Embrace the sophistication AI brings to post scheduling, but do so with your eyes wide open, your mind sharp, and your strategy as flexible as it is informed. With AI as your compass, you're poised not just to reach your audience but to connect with them when they're most receptive—turning mere moments into meaningful engagement.

Chapter 7:
Engaging with Your Audience via AI

In the art of digital engagement, there is a fine line between noise and resonance, and with the advent of artificial intelligence, we've been handed an orchestra. Engagement is not merely about talking at your audience; it's about talking with them, understanding their nuances, and creating a symbiotic digital relationship. Transitioning smoothly from a world where content distribution ruled, we must now embrace the power of AI to not only reach but deeply connect with our communities. Weaving AI into the fabric of audience interaction, chatbots and tailored AI interactions become our emissaries, creating a level of personalized experience that's scalable, yet feels intimate and responsive.

Enhancing User Experience with Chatbots and AI Interactions

In the exhilarating landscape of social media, where every click, like, and comment propels brands closer to their audience, AI stands as a transformative ally. The introduction of chatbots and AI interactions is not just a trend—it's revolutionizing the way we connect and communicate online. By incorporating AI-driven solutions, marketers and content creators are not only enhancing user experience but truly reinventing it.

Chatbots, equipped with ever-evolving AI, are the digital conversationalists of the new era. They seamlessly engage users with instant, tailored responses, mimicking human-like interactions but with a delightful twist of efficiency that no human can match. These upbeat digital assistants are sophisticated, often charming, and tirelessly adaptive, which makes the user journey fluid and pleasant.

The brilliance of leveraging AI interactions lies in personalization. Imagine a tool capable of understanding the distinct tastes and preferences of innumerable users and then, like an attentive concierge, providing recommendations that hit the mark with stunning accuracy. That is the sheer power of AI in enhancing the user experience—it knows, sometimes better than we know ourselves.

A one-size-fits-all approach is a bygone strategy; we live in an age of customization. Audiences crave experiences that echo their unique journey. Chatbots fortified with AI can analyze past interactions, browsing history, and social media behavior to present options that resonate deeply with individual users, amplifying their satisfaction and fostering brand loyalty.

Speed, too, is of the essence. Users no longer tolerate waiting for answers, and chatbots don't ask them to. They operate on the currency of immediacy—streamlining customer service by providing quick answers to frequently asked questions, troubleshooting in real-time, and even escalating issues to human representatives when needed without missing a beat.

Yet, at the heart of AI interactions is empathy. The sophisticated algorithms powering these bots have transcended cold mechanical responses. They now conjure a sense of understanding and emotional intelligence, learning as they interact and refining the way they engage to make each conversation feel distinctly human and remarkably intuitive.

What's more, the integration of chatbots goes beyond customer service. You can deploy them across numerous marketing campaigns to engage users, collect invaluable data, and drive conversions with a finesse that was once unimaginable. From interactive quizzes to personalized shopping experiences, these chatbots are the new workhorses of digital strategy, and they're only getting smarter.

AI doesn't just augment the experience; it continuously enhances it. With each interaction, the AI grows wiser, mapping out user behavior and preferences, which, in turn, empowers content creators to tailor content with precision. It learns and evolves, ensuring that your digital presence is not stagnant but a living, breathing entity in the social media ecosystem.

Moreover, AI-driven chatbots humanize brands. By offering a conversational touch, they distill the essence of your brand's voice and personality into every text bubble. This subliminal messaging weaves a narrative that users connect with, transforming a simple chat into a memorable brand encounter.

The introduction of chatbots doesn't mean the displacement of human touch; it means its enhancement. By handling routine inquiries, AI frees up human capital to tackle complex, creative tasks. This symbiotic relationship between man and machine invites a landscape where creativity thrives unencumbered, and user satisfaction soars.

And let's not ignore the economic wisdom of incorporating AI interactions. With their ability to operate round the clock without fatigue, chatbots present an opportunity for cost efficiency that's hard to ignore. They provide superior service without the overhead costs associated with human staff, delivering ROI that readily impresses the most discerning financial eyes.

But challenges in implementing AI chatbots are as real as their benefits. The key is in their seamless onboarding, ensuring that the transition to an AI-assisted interface is smooth for both users and staff. Rigorous testing, fine-tuning responses, and preparing for every possible user scenario are critical steps in this journey.

One must tread the path of using AI in chatbots delicately, constantly ensuring that the humanity of your brand isn't lost in automation. An impeccable balance must be struck, where technology and human insight coalesce to script experiences that are wondrously personal and reflect a touch of genius only attainable by this grand collaboration.

The artful integration of AI into user interactions is not simply a task—it's a dance of algorithms and emotions, data and dreams. As we step into the future hand-in-hand with AI, the experiences we craft for our users will define the depth and breadth of our brands' digital horizons.

In conclusion, chatbots and AI interactions are not merely tools but vehicles of metamorphosis for the user experience. They're transforming the frontiers of engagement, personalizing communication, and propelling your brand into a future where every digital interaction is an opportunity to connect, charm, and convert. Embrace the power of AI, and marvel as it crafts not just content but experiences that linger long after the screen dims.

Building Community with AI-Driven Engagement Techniques

As we edge further into a digitally connected world, the art of community building has transformed. Artificial intelligence now stands at the frontier of this evolution, presenting content creators with innovative strategies to engage with their audiences like never before. This transition to AI-driven engagement is not just innovative—it's revolutionary, reshaping how connections are forged and maintained in the virtual space.

The linchpin of a robust online community lies in sustained, dynamic interaction. AI, with its remarkable analytical abilities, brings precision to engagement strategies by tailoring interactions to community preferences and behaviors. It's about understanding not just who your audience is, but how they move, speak and connect.

Imagine an environment where conversations are not just reactive but predictive. AI-driven tools enable us to anticipate community needs, providing insights and actions that foster a proactive engagement approach. This nuanced understanding of the community's pulse can turn sporadic interactions into ongoing dialogues that build trust and loyalty.

Using AI to segment your audience is the first step in crafting personalized experiences. With the ability to parse through vast swaths of data, AI identifies patterns and segments audiences accordingly, ensuring that the content each member receives speaks directly to their interests and needs—a fundamental step in nurturing an engaged community.

Content creators can leverage AI-generated insights to tailor engagement activities, such as AMAs (Ask Me Anything) sessions, polls, and quizzes that resonate with community interests. AI's role here is to provide a decision-making base, processing engagement data to refine and optimize future interactions within the community.

Furthermore, AI can take immediate actions based on user behavior. Picture a community member posting about a service issue; AI can instantly recognize this and trigger a support response, seamlessly integrating customer service within the community experience. This responsiveness elevates the community beyond a platform for discussion, transforming it into a space for support and resolution.

The engines of AI can also power user-generated content campaigns, spurring innovation and creating a sense of ownership among community members. By analyzing trends and user involvement, AI can stimulate user content creation that is aligned with the community's enthusiasm, further strengthening the communal bond through shared contribution.

Leaderboards, rewards, and recognition systems driven by AI not only promote healthy competition but also celebrate active members, incentivizing their involvement and nurturing ambassadors for the brand. These techniques can fine-tune community sentiment, steering it towards positive and sustained engagement.

Personalized content delivery, facilitated by AI, ensures that every community interaction is relevant and timely. By analyzing when and how community members interact with content, AI-assisted algorithms can optimize the timing and format of posts to maximize engagement and community satisfaction.

When it comes to community moderation, AI tools act as vigilant gatekeepers, maintaining the integrity of the space. They monitor discussions in real time, managing harmful content and ensuring that exchanges adhere to community guidelines. This protective layer supports an environment where open, respectful, and constructive discussions flourish.

Above all, AI-driven engagement equips content creators with a powerful storytelling tool. It sifts through the noise to reveal the narratives that captivate your audience, allowing for storytelling that's not just compelling, but also contextual and deeply engaging.

Integrating AI in community building also means staying on the cutting edge of technological advancements. Content creators must remain agile, avid learners ready to wield new AI capabilities that are constantly emerging. This dedication ensures that the strategies evolve at the pace of the community's needs.

As we harness the power of AI for community engagement, the focus must remain steadfast on the human aspect. It's about augmenting the human touch with the efficiency of AI, not replacing it. Personal connections formed within the community should feel genuine, with AI working quietly in the background to enhance those relationships.

To measure the impact of AI on community engagement, analytics and reporting are indispensable. They provide a clear picture of engagement levels, the health of the community, and areas requiring improvement. Leveraging AI for these analytics can reveal trends that might escape the human eye, enabling strategists to make informed, data-driven decisions for the community's betterment.

The ultimately successful community is one that grows organically around shared interests and values, empowered by AI-driven engagements that facilitate meaningful connections. It's crucial for content creators to adapt to these AI advancements with a blend of creativity, empathy, and strategic thinking to build dynamic, thriving online communities.

Chapter 8:
Measuring Success: AI-Driven Analytics and Reporting

As we emerge from the nuanced discourse of AI-fuelled engagement tactics, the logical progression leads us to a realm where the fruit of our strategic labors can be quantified. In Chapter 8, we delve headfirst into the vital arteries of metrics that pulse with the lifeblood of data-driven decision-making. The power of AI-driven analytics lies in its ability to transform raw data into actionable insights, allowing marketers to stride beyond the traditional gut-based approach and into an era of enlightened strategy refinement. Key performance indicators become the stalwart guides in this journey, pointing towards the successes and signaling the missteps. But it's not just about numbers; it's about interpreting the narratives that these numbers spin, adapting your strategy to the ever-changing rhythm of audience behaviors. Each click, share, and engagement paints a picture of your campaign's performance, teaching you to dance to the beat of what truly resonates with your audience. This is where success isn't just measured but also understood and enhanced, day by day, piece by piece. The discussions herein aren't just aimed at helping you read reports; they're designed to embed within you the acumen to ask the right questions, challenge the expected results, and pivot with precision. You'll emerge not just with a grasp of analytics but with the wisdom to wield them as a tool sharpening the edge of your competitive position.

Key Metrics for AI-Assisted Campaigns

Understanding the impact of AI on your social media campaigns hinges not just on intuition but on hard data. Consider metrics as beacons that light the path to what's working or burning bright with the need for change. Let's dive into the key metrics that can help you navigate these waters with the precision of a seasoned captain.

First on our radar is **engagement rate**. This golden metric is the heartbeat of your campaign's success. AI can optimize your content creation and ensure you're hitting the mark but are your followers biting the bait? Look beyond likes; examine comments, shares, and even the nature of the interactions. Are they positive, negative, or indifferent? AI analytics can dissect these interactions to provide you with a granular understanding.

Next, we can't talk about engagement without mentioning **click-through rate (CTR)**. It's a telling sign of whether your message compels action. AI tools can predict and test different calls-to-action, so when your CTR improves, you'll know that AI is not just fluff—it's working in your favor.

Let's pivot to **conversion rate**. Beyond engagement, conversions tell you who's taking the plunge from casual observer to active participant or customer. AI-assisted campaigns should ideally lead to higher conversion rates through targeted content and personalized user journeys crafted with the insights from advanced analytics.

Retention is the backbone of any brand's online community. Monitor the **customer retention rate** to gauge the stickiness of your social content. AI can tailor this content to increase repeat interactions, but only clear metrics can illustrate the longevity of your audience's commitment.

Cut through the noise by analyzing **reach** and **impressions**. Are your carefully crafted messages achieving the intended spread? AI can magnify the reach by determining the optimal times for posting and identifying the most resonant content, but it's the actual numbers that will tell you if your voice is being heard across the digital expanse.

With AI, you also have the power to dive into **consumer sentiment analysis**. This advanced metric deciphers the emotions behind user responses, giving you a nuanced perspective on how your brand is perceived. It's not simply about counting smileys versus frowns; it's about understanding the emotional impact your content creates.

Don't overlook the importance of **lead generation**. Quality leads are the lifeblood of any marketing strategy. AI helps refine target demographics and improve lead generation tactics, but real success is measured by the growth in qualified leads that have a genuine interest in your offering.

The **share of voice** is a pivotal metric that quantifies your brand's visibility in the market. It reveals how your messaging competes with the chatter. The AI's ability to adjust strategies in real time based on trending data feeds into this metric, positioning your brand in the limelight it deserves.

Scrutinize your **cost per acquisition (CPA)**. AI can streamline your marketing efforts, potentially leading to a lower CPA. This metric will show you the efficiency of your spending—whether AI is helping your budget stretch further and attract customers more cost-effectively.

Customer Lifetime Value (CLV) is a metric that forecasts the net profit attributed to the entire future relationship with a customer. AI can personalize experiences, predict customer behaviors, and optimize lifecycles, but CLV will show you the tangible long-term gains of an AI-integrated strategy.

Examine the efficacy of **content virality** through metrics like social shares and the velocity at which content spreads. AI tools can predict potential virality, but the actual measurements confirm whether your content has the wings to rise above the digital din.

The **net promoter score (NPS)** is a beloved metric that has stood the test of time. It determines the likelihood that your customers will recommend your brand to others. AI can enhance customer satisfaction rates, but the NPS gives you the cold, hard numbers on your brand's evangelists.

Time on site and **page views** also offer deep insights. They become even more telling when AI-driven A/B testing is applied to differentiate between what holds a user's attention and what sends them scurrying away. By rigorously analyzing variations in these metrics, AI can systematically improve user engagement.

In conclusion, this kaleidoscope of metrics—engagement rate, CTR, conversion rate, retention, reach, sentiment analysis, lead generation, share of voice, CPA, CLV, content virality, NPS, and time on site—when viewed through the lens of AI, can pivot from plain data to a strategic masterpiece. AI-driven analytics weave these various strands of feedback into a coherent tapestry that tells the story of your campaign's success or offers a roadmap for course correction. Keep your eyes on these numeric narratives, for they wield the power to transform the fortunes of your brand in the bustling bazaar that is social media.

Interpreting Data and Adapting Strategies

The landscape has been surveyed; the mountains of data have been mined. Though it might seem like claiming victory is just a matter of reading a report, the reality is that interpreting AI-driven analytics and subsequently adapting strategies is an art form as much as it is a science. In the bustling world of social media, data isn't just numbers and charts; it's the voice of your audience, the reflection of your content's impact, and the signposts for your strategic journey ahead.

When those sleek spreadsheets and dashboards grace your screen, brimming with metrics, it's easy to become overwhelmed. But take heart; the key to unlocking these cryptic codes lies in distinguishing the signal from the noise. No matter how sophisticated artificial intelligence tools become, they serve up their bounty to human intellect, for it is the discerning marketer who reads between lines of data to pinpoint trends brewing beneath the surface. It is you who will connect the quantitative leaps with the qualitative insights, crafting a story from statistics that will guide your next move.

For instance, let's take engagement rate – a stalwart of social media metrics. AI's refined algorithms calculate this with finesse, taking into account likes, shares, comments, and more. Yet, what does a spike in engagement truly signify? Is it a reflection of content resonance, or perhaps the serendipity of timing? Here, critical thinking paired with AI's deep-dive data dissection illuminates the path forward: if a particular type of content perpetually outperforms the rest, it's a flare shot into the sky, signaling where to aim your creative efforts.

Interpretation, though, is more than recognizing what works. It is equally about identifying what doesn't. Negative feedback, while less pleasant, is an equally instructive facet of the analytics jewel. Decreasing follower growth or a high unfollow rate can seem alarming, but these are not just metrics of despair; they are opportunities for recalibration wrapped in warning tape. AI tools are impartial judges; they court no favor and disdain embellishment. It's your role to decode their unbiased findings and pivot before the ground gives way.

A dynamic strategy is one that breathes in response to the data it is fed. No campaign is set in stone, just as no social media landscape remains static. Recognize that adapting your tactics is not evidence of failure but of intelligent design. An AI-driven approach affords you a bird's-eye view of the terrain, so whenever the winds of social sentiment change, you can adjust your sails accordingly, with precision and confidence.

Cross-referencing data across different platforms facilitates a holistic perspective. If AI uncovers that certain content flourishes on one platform but flounders on another, it's a prompt to tailor your content to the unique ecosystems where your audience dwells. AI-driven analytics don't just offer reports, they serve as a lighthouse, guiding your content ship safely among the array of social media channels.

Data timelines also reveal patterns that might otherwise remain masked. A content series may start slow, but if the AI analysis shows incremental growth, patience and perseverance become your mantras. Just as a gardener wouldn't yank a seedling out of the soil for failing to be a tree, don't dismiss a slow-moving campaign if the data speaks of gradual success.

Segmentation is another crucial angle. Through the lens of AI, demographics, interests, and behaviors are dissected with surgical accuracy. This isn't just about appealing to the masses but speaking directly to niche corners of your audience. When you customize your content to resonate with these specific segments, you're not just casting a net – you're using AI as your sonar to fish where the fish are.

Moreover, adopting a test-and-learn approach is essential. AI tools can simulate and predict outcomes based on historical data and emerging patterns, but they cannot account for the caprice of human nature. Be audacious in your experimentation, be methodical in your testing, and behold as data transforms into your greatest teacher. What holds the day may not be the brightest idea but that which was honed to perfection through relentless testing and adaptation.

When interpreting your social AI data, remember that context is your ally. A sudden drop in engagement might not spell doom if it corresponds with broader market trends or seasonal shifts. AI can sift and sort, but you cast the narrative that gives meaning to the metrics. Use context to understand not just when and what, but why changes occur.

Finally, in the alchemy of interpreting data and adapting strategies, reflection is paramount. Every analysis should end with you looking back at your initial hypotheses and goals. Was the target missed because it was unfeasible or because the strategy was off-course? AI reports are more than final statements; they are breadcrumbs leading back to your starting point, showing where you strayed and where the path was true.

Cultivate agility in your plans. The digital realm is notorious for its rapid evolution, and what's relevant today might be archaic tomorrow. Use AI-driven analytics as your constant, adapting your strategies with the ebb and flow of the data tide. Mastery comes not only from learning how to read the charts but from sailing the swells with finesse and foresight.

As you forge ahead, arm yourself with the knowledge that every byte of data is a building block for your next breakthrough. It's up to you to piece together the puzzle in a way that tells a compelling story, resonates with your audience, and progresses your brand towards its zenith.

Interpreting data and adapting strategies is an ongoing process; one that beckons a blend of intuition, analytical thinking, and above all, the courage to evolve. Embrace it, and you'll find your path lined with insights that transform obstacles into stepping-stones, leading you to the pinnacle of social media success.

Chapter 9:
Ethical Considerations in AI Content Creation

As we turn the page from exploring data-driven decision making to the moral fabric underpinning our AI tools, we delve into a conversation that can't be shuttered behind the scenes. Ethical considerations in AI content creation are paramount; they shape the trust and credibility we foster with our digital constituents. At the heart of this chapter lies the delicate balance of innovative automation and the humane touch—the acknowledgement that while AI simplifies the complex, it should elevate, not erode, the ethical standards we hold dear. We investigate how biases can creep into algorithmic decisions, potentially skewing the narratives we weave, and we address the conundrums surrounding intellectual property in an era where creation blurs with curation. As architects of tomorrow's narratives, it is our responsibility to ensure the bedrock of our digital strategies is solid, sculpted from the finest ethical materials, ensuring that as our content reaches new heights, it stands on a foundation unyielding in its integrity.

Understanding AI Bias and Ethical Content

In this transformative digital age, where artificial intelligence shapes the contours of social media landscapes, we must address the elephant in the room—AI bias and its implications for ethical content. While these intelligent systems promise unparalleled personalization and efficiency, they also carry the risk of amplifying existing prejudices, as they learn from datasets that may be skewed by historical inequities. Crafting content that transcends bias and upholds the tenets of fairness requires a conscious approach to the data we feed our algorithms. It's about dissecting the DNA of AI decisions and ensuring diversity within the training sets, thus fostering an environment where every piece of content is a reflection of a just and equitable worldview. Let's harness the formidable power of AI, not only to captivate and engage but also to uphold the highest ethical standards, setting a precedent for content that's as conscionable as it is cutting-edge.

Navigating the Gray Areas of AI Intellectual Property

In the enthralling tapestry of social media content creation, artificial intelligence (AI) serves as an innovative weaver, blending creativity with efficiency to produce a vibrant array of digital experiences. As content creators employ AI to elevate their narratives, a complex question unravels: Who holds the rights to the intellectual property generated by AI? This puzzlement is the foundation of the murky domain of AI-generated intellectual property.

In this densely woven domain, understanding the nuance between inventiveness and the guiding hand of a machine is key. As the distinction blurs, it beckons the need for marketing professionals and digital strategists to navigate this terrain with insight and foresight. It's critical to peer into the legal framework that currently blankets this space with a patchwork of regulations and precedents, placing a premium on more than just understanding—but effectively maneuvering around—the intellectual property implications of AI-engendered content.

First and foremost, it's essential to recognize that as of now, the legal landscape treats AI as a tool rather than an independent creator. This means that the intellectual property rights of work produced with the assistance of AI typically vest with the human operator—the one who initiates and guides the AI. However, this straightforward principle is constantly challenged by the increasing autonomy and creativity of AI systems.

Cases where AI ventures beyond routine automation and actually contributes novel elements to a piece of content are where lines start to blur. It sparks critical questions: If an AI, fed with swathes of data, generates a unique piece of content, is its human controller truly the 'author'? This question is not merely academic, it has real-world implications for content creators looking to secure the rights to their AI-assisted work.

Consideration of the country-specific laws can lead to vastly different interpretations and applications. In some jurisdictions, the rigidity of traditional authorship concepts can be at odds with the fluidity of AI-driven creation. Globally, there's no consensus yet, which pitches creators at the heart of a legal quagmire. They must diligently track the evolution of laws in their local domains as well as international rules that might influence their rights.

As AI systems grub and digest massive datasets to output an array of engaging content, the question of data provenance comes to the fore. The initial datasets fed to AI—can they be free from copyright restrictions? Could the use of copyrighted material in training AI inadvertently lead to infringement? Content creators need to be vigilant in ensuring that the data used to train AI does not encroach on existing copyrighted material, lest their AI-powered content be tainted with liability.

Moreover, creators should be proactive in establishing robust and transparent arrangements when working with AI. This means drawing clear lines in contracts about the nature of the AI's contribution to the creative process. Doing so will mitigate potential legal disputes over ownership and rights. By explicitly attributing contributions, they can clarify the scope of their intellectual property and secure it more confidently.

Diving deeper into the quagmire, licensing becomes a pivotal lynchpin. Since AI-driven content often necessitates complex licensing arrangements, creators must be adept at negotiating terms that allow the fullest exploitation of their work while remaining within the boundaries of legality. This necessitates an understanding of licensing agreements that not only account for current laws but are also visionary enough to anticipate future changes.

Transparency too is a bulwark in this endeavor. Creators should strive to disclose the role of AI in their content creation process, which can help in setting a standard for the industry and lay the groundwork for a more definitive future regulatory framework. Additionally, such candor could be vital in sustaining the trust of their audience and maintaining the integrity of their work.

As the thick foliage of AI intellectual property issues looms, creators must educate themselves continuously. Leveraging industry groups, legal counsel, and staying abreast of new developments in case law is essential. Only through such relentless quest for knowledge can one adeptly pivot strategies and protect their creative ventures.

A strategy of adaptation can't be understated; creators should consider revisiting and revising their governance and compliance protocols regularly. The aim is to ensure that they are consistently aligned with the latest legal interpretations and are risk-averse in their approach to licensing and copyright.

While considering the promise and pitfalls of AI in content creation, creators must anchor themselves in a proactive stance—advocating for a clear and fair legal rubric that will foster creativity and innovation while still protecting the interests of genuine content creators. Their voice and experience can be a guiding lamplight for policymakers to draft laws that complement the advancements in AI.

In the quest to create engaging content in this digital era, as marketers and content creators sail through the gusts of AI's capabilities, they must also be the custodians of the intellectual treasures they craft. The recognition of AI's role in content creation, while essential, shouldn't obscure the significance of human ingenuity—at the end of the day, it is their vision that sparks the creation process, and their craft that molds AI's raw output into forms that resonate with the human experience.

The mists of uncertainty surrounding AI-generated intellectual property may seem daunting, but with thoughtful navigation, there lies an ocean of opportunity. For those who engage with AI as the powerful tool it is—remember to tread with intention and clarity, for in the balance of creativity and caution, the masterpiece of your digital narrative awaits.

Chapter 10:
Future-Proof Your Skills:
Staying Ahead in the AI Curve

In an ever-accelerating digital world, the frontier of artificial intelligence is an unbeaten path lined with untold possibility. As you've now understood the formidable force AI wields in social media dynamics, your journey must evolve to embrace the pulse of technological innovation. Keeping your skills sharply honed on the AI curve isn't just savvy—it's survival. In this chapter, we don't just theorize about distant horizons; we dig our heels into the shifting grounds of today's technological landscape and crystal-gaze into AI's latest trends in a way that's grounded, actionable, and unyieldingly forward-thinking. The capacity to adapt is integral to success, demanding that you grasp emerging technologies with an acrobat's balance and a strategist's mind. This isn't just about being conversant with the cutting-edge—it's about becoming an architect of change, shaping your capacity to create content that not merely rides the wave but commands the tides of tomorrow's AI developments.

AI Trends to Watch

As we navigate the ever-expanding sea of artificial intelligence, it's critical to identify the beacons that signal future trends. They guide us through the murky waters of technological innovation and into the harbor of success. One such trend that's gaining momentum is the rise of generative AI. Imagine software that doesn't just learn but creates - from articles to images, forging content that's not only original but also engaging and tailored to your audience's preferences. It's revolutionary and is rewriting the playbook for content creators and digital strategists.

The mastery of natural language processing is another trend stepping into the limelight. The sophistication of AI in understanding context, humor, and subtleties in language has made significant leaps. This implies that AI-powered content won't just be accurate; it will resonate on a human level, cracking the code of emotional engagement through digital screens.

Visual content creation with AI is not lagging behind. AI's ability to process and generate complex visual media is blossoming. This means that very soon, the static images you're used to could transform into dynamic visuals. They will captivate your audience, tell a compelling story, and offer immersive experiences just with the click of a button. This development has the potential to elevate branding and storytelling to exhilarating new heights.

Let's not underestimate the momentum behind voice search optimization and voice-generated content. With devices becoming more conversational, AI's role in optimizing for voice search is crucial. Content creators need to weave this into their strategies to ensure that their brand voice is heard, quite literally, above the rest.

With AI, the focus on content personalization has sharpened like never before. The tools at our disposal are getting better at predicting user behavior and crafting messages that feel like they're penned by a close friend rather than a corporation. This transition to hyperpersonalized content is not just a phase – it's the foundation for the user experience of tomorrow.

Ethical AI is another dimension rapidly coming into the spotlight. As these tools grow more integral to our content creation workflows, scrutinizing their algorithms for bias and ensuring transparency becomes paramount. This evolution is bound to shape the industry's approach to content creation – anchoring it in responsibility as much as innovation.

Another trend gathering steam is the democratization of AI. Sophisticated content creation tools that were once the exclusive domain of large corporations with deep pockets are becoming more accessible. They're cropping up in the market at price points that allow small businesses and individual creators to ride the AI wave too.

The synergy between AI and the Internet of Things (IoT) is opening new frontiers. With IoT devices capturing real-time data, AI can analyze and use this information to produce content that's not just timely, but also hyper-relevant to the context in which it's consumed. It's a game-changer for engagement and user experience.

The rise of AI-powered chatbots capable of genuine conversation is transforming customer engagement. No longer the clunky, robotic voices of yore, these chatbots are fast becoming adept conversationalists, offering personalized interactions and support that are redefining customer service in the digital space.

Moreover, the evolution of AI in influencer marketing is an exciting frontier. Predictive analytics can now cast light on which influencer partnerships will be most fruitful, saving time and capital while increasing the effectiveness of marketing campaigns. This trend is key for strategists looking for a robust ROI on their influencer collaborations.

Blockchain technology, in concert with AI, is also on the rise. This synergy promises to forge new pathways for content verification, intellectual property rights, and secure distribution, assuring both creators and consumers that the content they're consuming or paying for is authentic and protected.

Real-time content optimization using AI doesn't just shape content after it's been posted. It now has the power to alter and serve different variations of content dynamically based on user interaction. This continual optimization loop can substantially amplify engagement and content performance metrics.

The emergence of AI in augmented reality and virtual reality spaces is crafting full-bodied digital worlds where content is not just seen or read, but experienced in three dimensions. For marketers, this trend presents a novel canvas painted with the brushstrokes of innovation and immersion.

Lastly, the proliferation of AI regulatory technologies is a trend to keep an eye on. As we dive into using these powerful AI tools, it's increasingly vital to understand and abide by the legal frameworks that govern them. This harmonizing of technology with compliance ensures that as content creators, we remain on the right side of the law.

Embracing these trends will secure not just relevance but reverence in an industry where staying ahead of the curve doesn't just maximize success, it defines it. The fusion of creativity, adaptation, and the astute utilization of these AI trends will craft the masterpieces of tomorrow's digital content landscape.

Adapting to Continuous Change in AI Technology

The landscape of AI technology is akin to an ever-growing organism, reaching new heights and evolving at a breathtaking pace. For the savvy marketer, digital strategist, or content creator, embracing this constant transformation isn't just beneficial; it's imperative to maintain a competitive edge. Adaptability, then, becomes a skill as critical as any technical know-how in your arsenal.

To thrive in an environment where AI is continuously redrawing the boundaries of possibility, it's essential to develop a mindset anchored in perpetual learning. Each stride in AI advancement serves up fresh tactics, insights, and tools that can power your social media content to new levels of engagement and effectiveness. Staying ahead means keeping your finger on the pulse of emergent AI technologies and understanding how they can be harnessed to shape narratives that resonate with your audience.

But how does one stay flexible and responsive in such a rapid-fire context? Building a framework for ongoing education is paramount. This involves regularly setting aside time to explore the latest AI offerings, whether through webinars, online courses, or peer-led workshops. Information is your ally, and cultivating a knowledge-seeking habit will ensure you're never left behind.

Integration of AI advancements should also be an iterative process, allowing for testing and learning. Merely jumping on the newest tool isn't enough; you need to critically assess its impact on your work. Start small, with pilot projects or A/B tests, to understand the real value of an AI feature or tool before fully committing to it. Use data and feedback to iterate and refine your approach continually.

Nurturing a network of peers and thought leaders who share your interest in the junction of AI and content creation can open up a world of insight. The wisdom of the crowd often illuminates paths you might not have found on your own, helping you navigate the maze of AI technology and its implications with greater confidence.

The evolution of AI is not just about technological advancements; it's also reshaping consumer expectations. Your audience now anticipates highly personalized and interactive experiences. Thus, staying informed about AI means understanding the nuanced ways it can elevate user experiences and meet audience demands. The stakes are high, but so are the rewards for those who can craft content experiences that are both technically innovative and deeply human at their core.

Moreover, develop agility in your work processes. AI tools can be disruptive, changing workflows and team dynamics. Address these shifts proactively by cultivating flexibility within your team. Encourage experimentation, and don't fear the initial disruptions that new AI integrations can cause. Over time, these will smooth out, leading to improved productivity and content quality.

In the continuously changing AI landscape, introspection is a valuable tool. Regularly take the time to reflect on your strategies and processes: which AI tools are delivering results, and which are more hype than helpful? Keep your strategies dynamic, and don't hesitate to pivot when necessary. Staying nimble allows you to capitalize on AI's true potential without being waylaid by its pitfalls.

With AI's rapid advancement, ethical considerations grow ever more crucial. As you adapt to new technologies, ground yourself in ethical practices that respect privacy, transparency, and fairness. AI's power must be matched with responsibility, and staying ahead means leading with integrity as much as it does with innovation.

Remember that AI is a supplement to human creativity, not a replacement. As you adapt, focus on developing the uniquely human skills that AI can't replicate—empathy, strategic thinking, and creative storytelling. These will remain your competitive advantages, no matter how sophisticated AI technology becomes.

Anticipating future trends is also a fundamental part of adaptation. Look not only to current technologies but also to what's on the horizon. A forward-thinking mentality can help you prepare for the next wave of AI advancements, ensuring you're ready to embrace them when they arrive.

Lastly, remember that AI is not an end in itself, but a means to achieving your goals. Keep your objectives crystal clear, and continually re-evaluate how AI technology serves those aims. If an AI solution doesn't enhance your ability to connect with your audience or drive campaigns, it might not be the right fit for you.

Adapting to the continuous change in AI technology isn't simply a challenge; it's an exciting opportunity. By committing to ongoing learning, fostering adaptability, and focusing on human-led creativity, you'll not only stay ahead in the AI curve but also chart a course for unparalleled content creation that resonates in the digital era. It's through this lens of possibility and optimism that the future of AI in content creation should be viewed—an era of untapped potential at your fingertips.

Embrace change. Be curious. Stay creative. Together, these tenets will serve as your north star in the vibrant, ever-evolving cosmos of AI technology. Success in this dynamic realm is there for the taking, for those who choose to continuously evolve with it.

Chapter 11:
Creating Viral Content
with AI Assistance

Viral content isn't just stumbled upon—it's sculpted with precision, insight, and a touch of digital alchemy. Harnessing the power of AI, today's content creators can charge their narratives with irresistible hooks engineered to captivate the collective psyche. In this chapter, we explore the fusion of AI's analytical prowess with human creativity to craft content that doesn't just reach audiences but resonates with them on a seismic level. By delving into the science of virality, we unearth the patterns that make content stick and spread like wildfire. AI tools now shoulder the heavy lifting of data crunching, freeing up your mind to marry trends with timeless truths, fashioning posts that don't just fade into the digital ether but spark conversations, drive engagement, and catapult your brand into the spotlight.

The Science Behind Virality and AI's Role

The quest for virality is akin to finding the Holy Grail in the digital content realm; it can catapult a brand into the stratosphere but elude even the most seasoned content creators. At its core, content goes viral when it triggers an emotional response, resonates with a wide audience, and compels that audience to share it. This chain reaction isn't just serendipity—it's a science that we're beginning to decode with cutting-edge artificial intelligence. AI's role in this phenomenon is potent and multifaceted. It diligently analyzes vast pools of data to unearth patterns of human behavior, maps out the nuances of network dynamics, and predicts what content is poised to resonate with audiences. By harnessing the power of machine learning, AI dissects and assembles the elements of virality, enabling creators to concoct content with the perfect blend of relevance, timing, and appeal that's necessary to start a digital wildfire, fostering an alchemy of storytelling and technology that's primed to command the digital stage.

Crafting Shareable Content Using AI Insights

As we navigate the deep waters of the digital content sea, it's clear that creating content that sparks shares, likes, and conversations is the treasure every content creator seeks. Using AI insights to craft shareable content isn't just savvy; it's a game-changer that amplifies your message to unforeseen audiences. Yet, how does one weave the analytical prowess of AI into the fabric of content that resonates on a deeply human level?

As content creators, we must first grasp that AI is our ally in uncovering the enigmatic patterns of user engagement. AI tools dissect vast seas of data, revealing what content types, formats, and narratives stir the soul of your audience. Imagine knowing with precision which topics cause the most heartbeat skips, which images make eyes linger, or which headlines pull readers into a click. That's the power you wield when you let AI insights guide your content creation.

But let's demystify this further. When we speak of crafting shareable content, we're speaking of a narrative that's not just seen but felt. AI can identify the emotional undercurrents that make content stick. Emotional analytics, a tech marvel, evaluates reactions to content, guiding creators to evoke the right sentiments - be it joy, curiosity, or awe. This, however, doesn't dilute the creative element; it enriches it with direction and purpose.

Understanding your platform is paramount. Each social media channel has its unique language and cadence. AI-powered analytics dig into each platform's performance metrics, tailoring content that dances to the rhythm of that particular social stage. For example, AI might reveal that your Twitter audience thrives on wit and real-time commentary, while your Instagram followers yearn for visual storytelling.

The key to shareability lies in the art of storytelling. AI can suggest trending narratives or predict emerging stories, but it's the human touch that turns these suggestions into compelling tales. Use AI as a compass to navigate the narrative ocean, but let your creativity helm the ship. It's this synthesis of man and machine that creates stories that sail beyond the horizon of shareability.

Timing is not just a factor—it's a protagonist in the play of shareability. AI predictive analytics serve as a powerful oracle, unveiling when your audience is most receptive. Armed with this insight, you can schedule content for the moment it has the best chance to catch the wave of maximum engagement.

Now, don't forget the visuals—content's most captivating allies. AI-driven design platforms can analyze trends and user preferences, suggesting imagery, colors, and fonts that arrest the eye. Coupled with your understanding of visual harmony, AI's recommendations help construct graphics that are not only pleasing but persuasive.

Speaking of persuasion, headlines are the gatekeepers of engagement. AI tools that specialize in language processing can generate a variety of headlines designed to resonate with your audience and compel them to share. These suggested headlines are data-backed invitations to your content, engineered to maximize curiosity and click-through rates.

AI doesn't just predict; it learns. Machine learning algorithms refine their insights with every interaction, growing more attuned to what enchants your audience. As you implement AI suggestions and observe the results, the system updates its understanding, making your quest for shareability not a guessing game, but a strategic procession towards virality.

Localizing content is more than translation; it's about cultural resonance. AI's data-driven insights into regional preferences ensure that when your content travels, it speaks the local dialect of desire. By tailoring your message to align with local nuances, AI positions your content as a native in the hearts of a global audience.

No man is an island, and no content should exist in a vacuum. AI assists in identifying potential partners and influencers whose audiences might find your content shareable. Connecting with these nodes in the social network through collaborative AI-driven outreach can amplify your reach exponentially.

Moreover, shareable content must evolve. AI analytics provides real-time feedback, illuminating which aspects of your content ignite conversation and which fizzle out. This is not a cue for disappointment but an opportunity for rapid evolution, crafting your content to adapt to the ever-changing digital landscape with agility.

Crafting content that endures the test of shareability requires more than just a sprinkle of AI—it demands a harmonious blend. Your unique insights, your voice, and your brand's heartbeat can't be replicated by machines. AI serves as the spotlight, illuminating the path, but it's your humanity that lights up the content stage, capturing and reflecting the myriad facets of relatable, shareable experiences.

Contemplate the cross-pollination of AI-generated insights and human creativity as the soil from which the most shareable content grows. The content that thrives is content with roots in data but blossoms through the authenticity of human expression. It's this symbiotic relationship that molds shareable content into a tool that doesn't just reach audiences but resonates with them on a profound level.

In closing, let the deployment of AI in your content strategy be as intentional as the strokes of an artist's brush. Use the data, embrace the insights, and let the analytics shape your approach. But never lose sight of the ultimate goal: to connect, to engage, and to inspire action. That's the true essence of crafting shareable content using AI insights.

Chapter 12:
Monetizing AI-Generated Content

In the realm of AI-generated content, the keys to unlocking its economic potential lie in understanding the subtle art of monetization. This chapter delves into innovative revenue models tailored specifically for AI-created assets. As we unlock the doors to monetizing these digital masterpieces, it's crucial to comprehend the various streams through which your content can turn byte into bounty. Innovators in the field aren't just asking "Can AI help me create?" but are pushing the envelope to "How can AI help me earn?" By implementing smart AI deployment strategies, we're not only streamlining the content creation process but also maximizing return on investment in a landscape where every click counts. A kaleidoscope of possibilities emerges — from direct monetization channels to indirect revenue sources that amplify your earning potential while cementing your place as a frontrunner in the digital content marathon. In this era, it isn't just about making AI work; it's about making AI work for you economically.

Revenue Models for AI-Created Content

As we delve into the crux of monetizing AI-generated content, it's pivotal to understand the diverse revenue models that empower content creators to reap the benefits of their AI-crafted masterpieces. In this landscape, innovation is not a luxury—it's a necessity. And the propulsion of AI in the frontier of content creation has surfaced novel ways to generate revenue that merit keen exploration.

Subscriptions are a tried and tested model—paywalls carved from the virtual environment of content access. AI accelerates this model by customizing content offerings to individual preferences, thereby enhancing value and retention. Picture an AI churning analysis on trending topics and tailoring a newsletter that keeps subscribers hooked—now that's the kind of content worth paying for.

Licensing can also be modified in the context of AI-generated content. For example, a proprietary algorithm could allow creators to license unique content formats or automated storytelling templates, opening a revenue stream that capitalizes on innovation.

Ad-supported revenue models aren't left out of the AI revolution either. AI's predictive abilities can enhance targeting, pushing content that meshes so well with the audience's preferences that the click-through rates can soar. This refined targeting translates into higher ad revenues—an AI-amplified sweet spot for content creators and advertisers alike.

Transaction fees can be integrated into platforms where AI enables creative transactions. Envisage a marketplace for AI-designed digital assets; content creators could earn a commission for each purchase made through such AI-integrated platforms.

Affiliate marketing, too, finds new life with AI. By generating content that seamlessly integrates and recommends products, AI can dramatically improve conversion rates, fostering an environment where symbiotic relationships thrive between creators and the companies they affiliate with.

Donations and crowdfunding can adopt AI to tell a more compelling narrative. AI can analyze vast data sets to pinpoint the most effective way to appeal to potential donors, providing content creators with insights that can trigger generosity among audiences.

Then there's the dynamic world of virtual goods and currency. Through AI, virtual experiences can become even more engaging, prompting users to indulge in in-app purchases that enhance their interaction—all adding up to a lucrative aspect of content monetization.

Hardware bundling represents yet another facet, where AI-driven content is coupled with specific devices or software to incentivize purchases. Imagine AI-drawn artwork selling alongside high-end drawing tablets, creating a valuable bundle for consumers who are drawn to the exclusivity of AI-created work.

Personalized merchandise is a natural extension of AI's abilities. With AI-designed graphics, content creators can offer merchandise that feels more personal, tapping into the eagerness of audiences to own something uniquely 'them.'

Data monetization can be a gold mine too. AI-generated content provides a wealth of data about user preferences, and through careful, privacy-conscious strategies, this data can be utilized to inform decisions across a spectrum of industries.

Consulting services can emerge from the depth of AI expertise; creators who master AI-generated content can advise businesses on how to embed AI into their content strategy, creating a client base eager to harness the power of AI.

Invest in training and education—develop courses and tutorials that clarify the nuances of AI in content creation, offering a ladder for aspiring creators to climb towards expertise.

Finally, collaboration opportunities can be manifold with AI. Collaborating on sponsored content where AI aids in sculpting the narrative can lead to compelling and financially rewarding partnerships.

As AI continues to insinuate itself into every facet of content creation, the potential for monetization multiplies exponentially. It's about peering into the crevices of innovation, determining where AI can add value that's not just significant, but extraordinary. With every piece of content, you have the opportunity to deploy AI not just as a tool, but as a transformative force that reshapes the way we think about revenue in the realm of digital creation. Tap into this potential, and you'll unlock doors to monetization that might not yet have been imagined, catalyzing a new era of digital profitability and creative fulfillment.

Maximizing ROI with Smart AI Deployment

Step into a world where smart AI deployment can transform your content strategies into lucrative returns, creating ripples that convert into waves of engagement and conversion. The utilization of AI in content creation isn't just about keeping up with trends; it's about outpacing the competition with efficiency and finesse.

Every marketer dreams of a return on investment (ROI) that multiplies with each campaign. And while AI can seem like a magic wand for content creation, it requires strategy to master its potential. The key isn't just in deploying AI but in doing so with tactical precision that aligns with your brand's unique objectives.

First, if you're going to get serious about ROI, you've got to get up close and personal with your analytics. AI-generated content is more than just a set-and-forget tool; it's about continual adjustment and refinement. Use AI to segment your audience and tailor your approach. The improved targeting isn't just efficient; it's a goldmine for engagement.

The beauty of AI is in its scalability. Start small with pilot projects to test waters before going big. Use these projects to understand what resonates with your audience. Observe the engagement metrics, fine-tune your approach, and watch as these insights catapult your content's effectiveness into new realms.

Remember, data is your best friend. AI thrives on data; the more it has, the smarter it gets. Build robust data repositories that your AI tools can leverage to produce content that's not just good, but spot-on for driving conversions. This will ensure that your content isn't just speaking to your audience, but singing to them.

Invest in AI tools that offer integration capabilities. A fragmented approach can dilute your efforts. Opt for platforms that communicate with each other, turning disparate data points into a symphony of actionable insights. The interconnectedness will make your content strategy more cohesive and powerful.

It's not just about automation, it's about augmentation. Use AI to enhance the creativity of your team, freeing them from the mundane to focus on strategy and growth. The result? A team that's not bogged down by process but is energized by possibilities.

Sure, cost savings are fantastic, but what's even better? Revenue generation. AI can help personalize offers, optimize pricing, and even predict and tap into emerging trends, ensuring that your content isn't just seen — it's sold.

Your content is the bridge between your brand and your customers. Build it with AI, and you equip yourself with adaptive architecture that not just meets but anticipates customer needs. This isn't just content creation; it's content evolution.

Feeling overwhelmed? Take a breath. Start with clear, achievable objectives before integrating AI. The roadmap you create should include benchmarks for success and scalability that reflects your company's capacity for growth and adaptation.

Stay vigilant, though. AI isn't infallible. Establish a feedback loop between your AI outputs and human oversight to ensure quality control. The AI-human collaboration isn't just smart; it's essential for maintaining the authenticity of your brand.

Incorporate AI-driven A/B testing to optimize content efficacy. Tiny tweaks can lead to significant improvements in engagement and ROI. What's more, by embracing a test-and-learn approach, you solidify a culture of continuous improvement that keeps you ahead of the game.

Think lifetime value, not just one-off conversions. AI can help you craft stories that resonate through the noise, fostering a sense of community and loyalty that turns followers into advocates. The ROI on loyalty is exponential and timeless.

And don't forget about compliance and ethics; ensure your AI tools are aligned with legal guidelines and moral standards. This not only protects your brand but also establishes trust with your audience. In an era where trust is currency, this is an investment you can't afford to overlook.

Finally, always keep an eye on the horizon. The digital landscape is ever-changing, and your AI strategies must adapt accordingly. Embrace the fluidity of this technology, harness its full potential, and watch as your content becomes a beacon of innovation, driving ROI that surpasses all expectations.

Navigating the AI terrain is no casual stroll; it's an expedition of strategic exploration. In the saga of digital marketing, let smart AI deployment be your guiding star, illuminating the path to monetization through content that connects, converts, and ultimately, conquers.

Online Review Request for This Book

If you've found value in navigating the intersection of AI and social media content creation, and believe in empowering your digital strategy with cutting-edge insights, please consider leaving a review to help others discover the roadmap to enhancing their content with AI's revolutionary capabilities.

Social AI Revolution

Chapter 13:
The Ongoing Social AI Revolution

As we reach the culmination of our exploration into the transformative world of social AI, it's crystal clear that we're not just standing on the brink of change—we're in the midst of a sweeping revolution. The landscape of social media content creation, distribution, and management has been redrawn, now furnished with powerful tools augmented by artificial intelligence.

Content creators, marketers, and digital strategists now harness AI to construct more personalized, engaging, and relevant narratives. We've journeyed through the nuts and bolts of AI in social media, inspected the tools that reimagine the content creator's craft, and learned to navigate this terrain with forethought and strategy.

Embracing this change takes guts, paired with an unshakable commitment to continuous learning. AI won't replace us—it will amplify our ingenuity. You now understand that creating content in the AI era isn't just about churning out posts—it's about architecting experiences that grip the heart and spark the mind. From predictive analytics optimizing post schedules to chatbots offering bespoke user experiences, AI is our partner in this dance of digitized expression.

While we have delved into the science of virality and the art of engagement, remember that the human element remains central. AI provides the map, but your creativity is the compass that directs this complex journey. Social AI tools have evolved to understand nuances and user patterns, yet your role in interpreting and leveraging these findings is fundamentally irreplaceable.

Integrating AI into your social media strategies has been shown to yield quantifiable successes, yet this integration extends beyond metrics. It's about building a community, fostering real conversations, and sparking connections. The role of AI-driven analytics and reporting is to illuminate the path, guiding your strategies to resonate even more deeply with your audience.

AI's impact stretches further into the domain of content distribution, enabling your messages to find the right audiences at the right times. But let's be clear: it's not just what AI can do for you—it's what you can do with AI. Mastering these tools gives you a competitive edge, allowing you to wield time and precision as weapons in the saturated battleground of content.

Your journey through this book has likewise illuminated the dueledged sword of AI: its potential for bias and the ethical considerations we must vigilantly address. As creators, it's our duty to use AI responsibly, crafting content that does not discriminate but instead celebrates the diversity of the human experience.

And while the horizon is bright with the potential for AI-assisted campaigns, it's crucial to remember that with great power comes great responsibility. Always approach AI as a means of enhancing, not overshadowing, the authenticity of your brand message.

As the revolution continues, you're now equipped to future-proof your skillset. Stay agile, stay informed, and stay ahead of the curve. AI technology is in constant flux, and it's your adaptability that will mark your content and strategies as perennial—not ephemeral.

Through the lucrative realm of AI-generated content, you've discovered new revenue models and recognized the significant ROI that smart AI deployment can deliver. It's a dynamic fusion of creativity and algorithmic precision that must be finely tuned to hit that sweet spot—where content not only sings but also sells.

The ongoing social AI revolution is not a distant dream but today's vivid reality. It's a reality that you can shape, guide, and lead. Your journey with AI is bound to be as exhilarating as it is challenging—and as we draw this book to a close, let's remember that the end of one chapter signifies the beginning of another.

With the recommended AI tools and platforms at your fingertips, as detailed in Appendix A, and the glossary of terms to anchor your understanding, tap into the potential that beckons. The resources for continuous growth lie all around you, contained within the very fabric of our digital landscape.

The revolution isn't waiting for a signal; it's unfolding before your eyes. Its rhythm is set by the creators who dare to envision a future punctuated by the collaboration between machine intelligence and human creativity. So now, with strategies and tactics in hand, it's your turn to step forth and cast your presence into the boundless realm of the social AI revolution.

In your hands lies the power to create, to connect, to engage and to transform. Let your journey be marked by bold steps and brilliant victories. You are not just a participant in this revolution; you are its driving force.

As you turn this final page and look toward the horizon of your own endeavors, remember that the tools and strategies shared here are but a prologue to your story. How it unfolds from here is driven by your vision, your voice, and your verve. The ongoing social AI revolution awaits your contribution—make it count.

Appendix A:
Recommended AI Tools and
Platforms for Content Creators

In the fast-paced world of social media, staying ahead of the game is not just a matter of choice, but a competitive necessity. As we have navigated through the diverse landscapes of AI-driven content creation, strategy establishment, personalized marketing, and community engagement, it's become clear that the right set of tools can make or break your digital presence. Now, let's roll up our sleeves and dive into an arsenal of recommended AI tools and platforms that are designed to propel content creators into a future where creativity meets efficiency and analytics become the new muse.

Content Creation and Optimization Tools

When it comes to content creation, the goal is to strike a sublime balance between creativity and productivity. AI platforms can transform your content strategy with machine-driven insights and automation that empower your storytelling.

- **Writesonic** - This AI-driven writing assistant helps you craft compelling copy, from social media posts to blog articles, in a fraction of the time.

- **Grammarly** - Beyond mere spellchecking, Grammarly offers tone detection and style suggestions to enhance the readability and impact of your writing.

- **Canva's Magic Resize** - A feature within Canva that effortlessly adapts your visual content for different social media platforms to maintain brand consistency across all channels.

AI Analytics and Personalization Platforms

Understanding your audience is key to content that resonates. These platforms use AI to decipher the data, helping you to tailor content that hits home with your target demographic.

- **Pattern89** - Discover what creative elements work best for your brand with AI-driven recommendations to fine-tune your visuals.

- **Crisp** - Use this tool to harness the power of AI for real-time social media monitoring and audience analysis.

- **PaveAI** - Turn Google Analytics data into actionable insights with AI-driven reports that inform content strategies.

AI for Scheduling and Distribution

Distributing your content at the optimal time is crucial for maximizing reach and engagement. Automate your posting schedule with platforms that predict peak engagement periods.

- **Buffer** - Plan and publish your content with ease, and use the AI-powered analytics to measure performance and refine your posting strategy.

- **Hootsuite Insights** - Tap into advanced sentiment analysis and trend predictions while scheduling your content across multiple platforms.

Chatbots and AI Engagement Tools

Engaging with your audience doesn't have to be a round-the-clock job. AI-driven chatbots and tools provide personalized interactions, helping you build a community even while you sleep.

- **ManyChat** - Create AI chatbots for Facebook Messenger to engage your followers with personalized messaging sequences.

- **MobileMonkey** - An omni-chat platform that lets you build chatbots for SMS, Web Chat, and more, perfect for nurturing your audience across different touchpoints.

These tools are just a glimpse into the treasure trove of AI resources available for today's content creators. Harness the capabilities they offer, and you'll find the potential to not just ride the wave, but actually steer the course of your digital success. Keep in mind, though, these tools are like instruments in an orchestra — it's the masterful use and harmony that will create the symphony of impactful content. Dive in with an experimentation mindset, and watch as the power of AI amplifies your creativity, connects you with audiences, and optimizes your strategies for the cyberspace of tomorrow.

Glossary
of AI and Social Media Terms

As we embark on a journey of discovery where artificial intelligence meets social dynamics, it's paramount to arm ourselves with a clear understanding of terms that are critical to navigating this landscape. Here's our curated glossary, honed to empower you with key terminology at the intersection of AI and social media.

Algorithm

An **algorithm** is a set of rules or instructions given to an AI system to help it make decisions or perform tasks. In social media, algorithms decide what content appears in a user's feed, based on relevancy, engagement, and other factors.

Artificial Intelligence (AI)

Artificial Intelligence, often abbreviated as AI, refers to machines designed to mimic human cognitive functions like learning, problem-solving, and pattern recognition. In social media, AI can analyze large data sets, optimize content delivery, and personalize user experiences.

Chatbot

A **chatbot** is an AI software that can simulate a conversation with users through messaging platforms, websites, or mobile apps. They are often used for customer service or to provide users with real-time assistance.

Content Automation

Content Automation utilizes AI to generate content for various platforms without human intervention, saving time and resources while maintaining a consistent presence online.

Data Analytics

Data Analytics involves analyzing raw data to find trends and answer questions. The AI algorithms used in social media analytics provide invaluable insights into user behavior, campaign performance, and content engagement.

Deep Learning

A subfield of machine learning, **Deep Learning** is based on artificial neural networks. It's a key technology behind the most advanced AI applications, including speech recognition, translation services, and image recognition on social platforms.

Engagement Rate

The **Engagement Rate** is a metric used to gauge the level of interaction users have with content on social media, typically defined as the total number of engagements divided by the number of impressions or reach.

Machine Learning (ML)

A cornerstone of AI, **Machine Learning** allows systems to automatically learn and improve from experience without being explicitly programmed. It's used in social media for functions such as content recommendation and ad targeting.

Natural Language Processing (NLP)

Natural Language Processing or NLP is a branch of AI that gives machines the ability to read, understand, and derive meaning from human languages. It enables features like sentiment analysis and language translation on social media platforms.

Predictive Analytics

Predictive Analytics uses data, statistical algorithms, and machine learning techniques to identify the likelihood of future outcomes based on historical data. It's increasingly used to forecast trends and user engagement in social media.

Programmatic Advertising

Programmatic Advertising involves automated buying and selling of online advertising, which optimizes ad spend by targeting more specific demographics. AI is revolutionizing this field by enabling real-time bidding and optimization.

ROI (Return on Investment)

ROI measures the profitability of an investment, comparing the magnitude and timing of gains to the investment costs. In social media marketing, calculating ROI is essential to evaluate the performance and impact of campaigns run with the aid of AI technologies.

Sentiment Analysis

An application of NLP, **Sentiment Analysis** assesses the emotional tone behind a series of words to gain an understanding of the attitudes, opinions, and emotions expressed in an online mention or piece of content.

Equipped with this compass of terminology, you are better prepared to leverage the power of AI in your social media endeavors. Embrace these terms, incorporate them into your strategy, and witness a transformation in how content cultivates connections, and narratives propel digital interactions to new heights.

Appendix B:
Further Reading and
Resources for AI in Social Media

As you've delved into the transformative world of AI in social media, you've equipped yourself with valuable insights, case studies, and actionable strategies. But the journey doesn't end here. The landscape of artificial intelligence is ever-evolving, and staying informed is critical to maintaining your competitive edge. Below is a curated list of further reading and resources to keep you at the forefront of AI developments in social media.

Books

- *Artificial Intelligence for Marketing: Practical Applications* – An in-depth guide that walks through the practical side of using AI in marketing and helps to appreciate the analytical side of social media.

- *Predictive Marketing: Easy Ways Every Marketer Can Use Customer Analytics and Big Data* - This book serves as a resource to understand how predictive analytics applies to customer data, an aspect central to social AI.

Online Courses

- **Coursera's AI For Everyone** – Provides a non-technical introduction to AI concepts, potential, and implications for business strategy.

- **Udemy's Artificial Intelligence in Digital Marketing** – A course tailored for marketing professionals looking to leverage AI in their digital strategies.

Research Papers and Reports

1. "The Rise of AI in Social Media" by the Social Media Research Foundation – Explores the advanced AI applications in enhancing the user experience on social platforms.

2. "Ethical Implications of AI in Social Media Content Moderation" via IEEE – Discusses the moral considerations and guidelines for the application of AI in moderating content.

Podcasts and Webinars

- **The Marketing AI Show** – A podcast series dedicated to discussing how marketers and businesses can harness AI's power.

- **AI in Business** – Offers a variety of webinars and podcast episodes focused on the enterprise application of AI, including social media.

Communities and Forums

For those yearning for real-time discussions and the latest thoughts from peers, social media groups and professional forums are a treasure trove of knowledge. Platforms like LinkedIn have groups dedicated to AI in marketing, and Slack communities such as 'Marketers United' often have channels for discussing AI tools and tactics.

Industry Blogs and Websites

- **The AI in Marketing Blog** – Provides the latest news, insights, and trends about AI in the world of marketing.

- **Marketing AI Institute** – A go-to resource for articles, case studies, and industry reports on the intersection of marketing and AI tech.

Engage with these resources to fuel your intellectual curiosity and practical know-how. As your fluency in the AI domain matures, you'll discover opportunities to innovate and lead in crafting magnetic content that captivates and converts.

Remember, the scope of AI is vast, and its implications for social media and content creation are just beginning to surface. Keep exploring, learning, and applying new AI insights to your social media practices. Your future self—the one who stands on the cutting edge of AI and social media synergy—will thank you for the relentless pursuit of knowledge and mastery in this exhilarating digital playground.

www.ingramcontent.com/pod-product-compliance
Lightning Source LLC
Chambersburg PA
CBHW051207050326
40689CB00008B/1232